THE NEW BEST OF FINE WOODWORKING

Workstations
and Tool Storage

Workstations and Tool Storage

The Editors of
Fine Woodworking

The Taunton Press

The Taunton Press
Inspiration for hands-on living®

The Taunton Press, Inc., 63 South Main Street, PO Box 5506, Newtown, CT 06470-5506
e-mail: tp@taunton.com

Jacket/Cover design: Susan Fazekas
Interior design: Susan Fazekas
Layout: Cathy Cassidy
Front Cover Photographer: Matt Berger, courtesy *Fine Woodworking*,
© The Taunton Press, Inc.
Back Cover Photographers: (left) Mark Schofield, courtesy *Fine Woodworking*, © The
Taunton Press, Inc.; (top right) Michael Gellatly, courtesy *Fine Woodworking*, © The Taunton
Press, Inc.; (bottom right) Dean Della Ventura, courtesy *Fine Woodworking*, © The Taunton
Press, Inc.

The New Best of Fine Woodworking® is a trademark of The Taunton Press, Inc.,
registered in the U.S. Patent and Trademark Office.

Library of Congress Cataloging-in-Publication Data
Workstations and tool storage / the editors of Fine woodworking.
    p. cm. -- (The new best of fine woodworking)
  ISBN 1-56158-785-0
 1. Woodwork--Equipment and supplies--Design and construction. 2. Workshops--
Equipment and supplies--Design and construction. 3. Workbenches--Design and
construction. 4. Storage in the home. I. Fine woodworking. II. Series.
 TT186.W687 2005
 684'.08--dc22

                         2005004874

Printed in the United States of America
10 9 8 7 6 5 4 3 2 1

The following manufacturers/names appearing in *Workstations and Tool Storage* are trade-
marks: Bessey®, De-Sta-Co®, Deft®, Grainger, Jorgensen®, Lexan®, Masonite®, Pony®,
Oneida Air Systems™, Record®, Simpson Strong-Tie®, Skil®, Styrofoam®, Watco®

Working wood is inherently dangerous. Using hand or power tools improperly or ignoring
safety practices can lead to permanent injury or even death. Don't try to perform operations
you learn about here (or elsewhere) unless you're certain they are safe for you. If something
about an operation doesn't feel right, don't do it. Look for another way. We want you to
enjoy the craft, so please keep safety foremost in your mind whenever you're in the shop.

Acknowledgments

Special thanks to the authors, editors, art directors, copy editors, and other staff members of *Fine Woodworking* who contributed to the development of the articles in this book.

Contents

Introduction

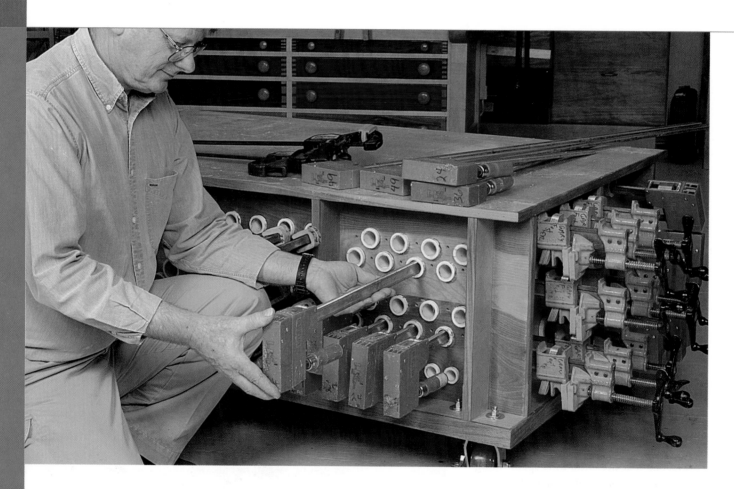

I have about 100 times more money invested in machines than in hand tools, but it's the hand tools I cherish most. Unlike a machine, a well-tuned hand plane or razor sharp chisel allows me to engage with wood in a personal, satisfying way. It's like driving a car vs. taking a walk. One method gets you there faster, but the latter allows you to see every ripple in the landscape.

Because of our fast-paced lives, we are thankful for machines; otherwise we would not do as many projects promised to our family or to our clients. But at some point all woodworking requires the use of some hand tools. Although you may not think of them as such, a ruler, a marking knife and a square are hand tools that are essential for layout as well as for machine setup. Knowing how to choose and use these tools will make you a better woodworker.

There are times when a handplane or chisel comes in handy, even if you work mostly with machines. Nothing pares an oversized tenon as accurately as a fine swipe across its cheek with a shoulder plane. To shape curvy parts like a ball-and-claw foot, you will need files, rasps and rifflers.

To do honest period work, you must cut your dovetails by hand. A fine-tooth saw and chisel will have to be employed and eventually sharpened to continue working. For certain details, like a narrow bead with a fine quirk or groove, you are best off making your own simple tool, a scratch stock.

These and other hand-tool articles are excerpted here from the pages of Fine Woodworking magazine. Once you start using more of these tools, you will see your work reach a higher level of refinement and realize that the extra time spent doing hand work is well worth every minute.

—Anatole Burkin, editor
Fine Woodworking

Fine-Tune Your Shop

BY JERRY H. LYONS

I had long dreamed of creating a perfect shop and using it to teach woodworking. I reached that goal six years ago when I purchased a 3,000-sq.-ft. ranch-style log cabin near my home. I converted that space into a shop where I do woodwork and offer classes on the subject.

Two words describe my workshop environment: clean and organized. As long as I can remember, I have needed a place for everything and everything in its place. I may have inherited the trait in school woodshop as the student who cleaned up after every class. Or perhaps my most recent career as a training and safety consultant, declaring the benefits of organization and systemization, has rubbed off on me.

Working in such a large space, I needed to keep hand tools organized, so I designed wall-mounted storage panels that make it easy to see and access tools. To make the workspace more efficient and adaptable, I also employ a variety of work tables and rolling carts, which do double duty as storage for project parts, related hardware, and even hand tools and jigs.

JERRY H. LYONS, who taught furniture making for 22 years, recently built his dream shop near Glasgow, Kentucky.

Assembly Cart Raises Work

This shopmade cart provides a comfortable working height (about 24 in.) and easy access to the back and sides of a large project, like this slant-top secretary (below). Also, the cart makes it easier and safer to roll a piece around my shop to take advantage of natural light. Both shelves are carpeted to protect the edges of the workpiece, and the lower shelf provides storage for components and hardware.

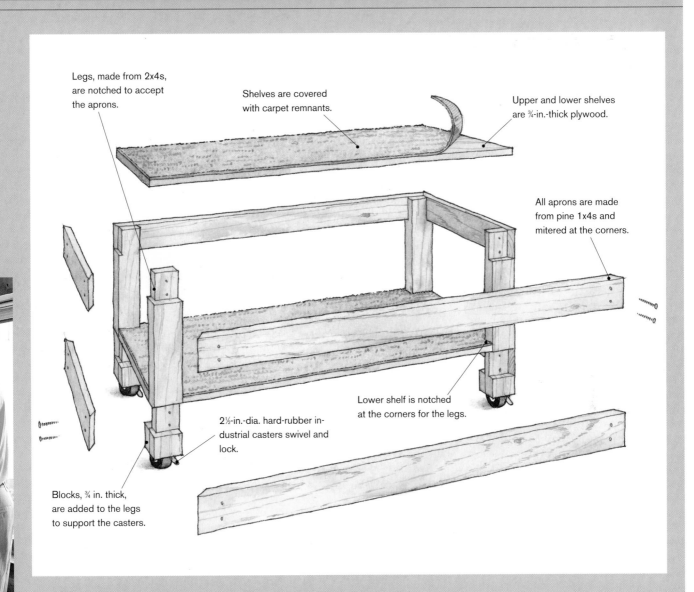

Legs, made from 2x4s, are notched to accept the aprons.

Shelves are covered with carpet remnants.

Upper and lower shelves are ¾-in.-thick plywood.

All aprons are made from pine 1x4s and mitered at the corners.

Lower shelf is notched at the corners for the legs.

2½-in.-dia. hard-rubber industrial casters swivel and lock.

Blocks, ¾ in. thick, are added to the legs to support the casters.

A SECRETARY ON THE MOVE.
This rolling cart allows Lyons to move work around the shop easily. It also keeps a piece at a comfortable working height, with access to all sides.

Wall Panels Organize Hand Tools

Like many woodworkers, I have lots of hand tools, and I want to be able to find a tool when I need it. I would rather spend my time working than looking. To organize my hand-tool collection, I built four tool panels near my workbenches. Each tool, regardless of its size, fits into its own space within one of these panels. The panel backs are made of ¾-in.-thick seven-ply oak plywood. The edging is solid oak rabbeted to receive the plywood and mitered at the corners.

To accommodate the needs of several students at once, all panels include common tools such as handsaws and planes. Whenever possible, I grouped tools—such as those for measuring, layout, and cutting—according to use.

I used a bandsaw, handplanes, and sanders to shape and mold each tool holder's unique configuration. I glued the tool holders in place and used screws and dowels for reinforcement.

DESIGNS ON DISPLAY. Lyons finds it helpful to keep plans for his current project displayed so that he can reference them easily without damaging them.

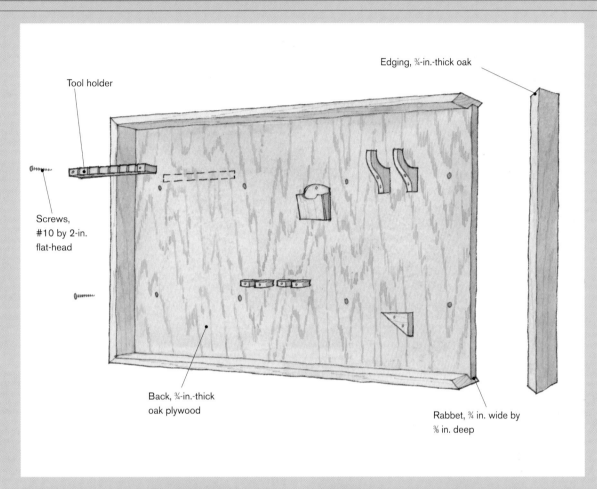

Tool holder

Edging, ¾-in.-thick oak

Screws,
#10 by 2-in.
flat-head

Back, ¾-in.-thick
oak plywood

Rabbet, ¾ in. wide by
⅜ in. deep

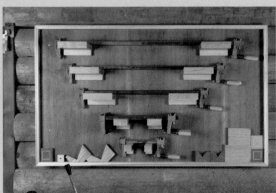

TOOLS ARE GROUPED ACCORDING TO USE. Layout tools and clamps are gathered on this tool panel.

A PLACE FOR EVERYTHING. Wall panels display hand tools, making them easy to find and access.

Clamping Table Tackles Glue-Ups

Gluing boards into panels often calls for at least three pairs of hands: one to keep the boards aligned, one to stop the clamps from falling over, and one to clean up the surplus glue. I solved this problem by making a dedicated clamping table.

The front and back edgings of the table are slotted to position I-beam bar clamps in an upright position. The tray below is covered with newspapers to catch glue squeeze-out. When done, I simply fold up the newspapers and discard them. This table also has a lower shelf to hold extra newspapers, several jigs, and occasionally used items.

I used a variety of scraps of plywood and solid stock to build the table, and then I painted the whole piece with leftover floor paint. This has the bonus of making glue cleanup easier. Size the table based on what scraps are available and the kind of work you do. My table is 30½ in. deep by 65 in. wide by 32 in. tall.

LESS STRESS AND LESS MESS. The slotted table frame holds clamps in position while you're gluing up boards. Any glue squeeze-out drips into the newspaper-lined tray.

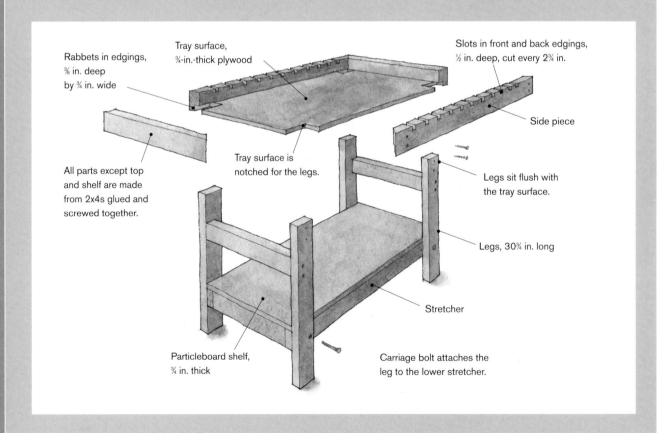

Rabbets in edgings, ⅜ in. deep by ¾ in. wide

Tray surface, ¾-in.-thick plywood

Slots in front and back edgings, ½ in. deep, cut every 2¾ in.

Side piece

All parts except top and shelf are made from 2x4s glued and screwed together.

Tray surface is notched for the legs.

Tray surface is notched for the legs.

Legs sit flush with the tray surface.

Legs, 30¾ in. long

Stretcher

Particleboard shelf, ¾ in. thick

Carriage bolt attaches the leg to the lower stretcher.

Mobile Table Serves Many Needs

This table is my heavyweight shop assistant: With a 1,000-lb. capacity, it never complains of backache; four wheels means it can move anywhere on the heavy-machinery floor; and because its wheels lock, the table never backs out when I need it most. The table is ⅛ in. below the height of the tablesaw to eliminate boards getting caught on it when they're being ripped. It can be positioned either lengthwise or widthwise, depending on the shape of the board being cut. It also makes a nice outfeed surface when you're planing long parts. In addition, it is a handy table for layout work as well as a good place to store clamps and other accessories. As with the clamping table, the dimensions of your table will differ based on your tools and the work you do.

A MULTIPURPOSE SUPPORT TABLE. This table can be wheeled to support operations at the tablesaw or the jointer, while the base stores clamps and jigs.

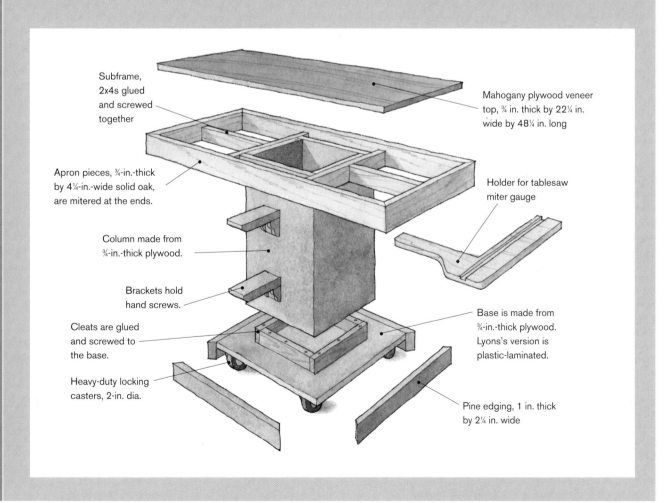

Subframe, 2x4s glued and screwed together

Mahogany plywood veneer top, ¾ in. thick by 22¼ in. wide by 48¼ in. long

Apron pieces, ¾-in.-thick by 4¼-in.-wide solid oak, are mitered at the ends.

Holder for tablesaw miter gauge

Column made from ¾-in.-thick plywood.

Brackets hold hand screws.

Base is made from ¾-in.-thick plywood. Lyons's version is plastic-laminated.

Cleats are glued and screwed to the base.

Heavy-duty locking casters, 2-in. dia.

Pine edging, 1 in. thick by 2¼ in. wide

Roll-Away Workshop

BY BILL ENDRESS

After many years living in central Florida, I received an invitation to relocate to Tucson, Arizona. Having been an active woodworker for 19 years, I placed adequate shop space high on my list when it came time to buy a home. While it would have been nice to find a house with a separate workshop, my wife and I settled on one with a spacious 23-ft. by 23-ft. two-car garage.

This presented me with a challenge: Create an efficient and comfortable workshop that could accommodate big projects but still make room for the family cars. So I began laying out all the basic requirements needed to share my tablesaw with my parking space.

The primary requirement was to keep at least one car in the garage at night, even if a half-finished project occupied floor space. The flexibility to park two vehicles in the garage on occasion also was essential. The challenge was balancing these requirements with the elements of a good shop: one that is attractive to work in, easy to clean, and has plenty of organized storage. My philosophy throughout was "a place for everything, and everything in its place."

Making Do with Limited Space

To have plenty of work space and be able to cut long boards with my radial-arm saw, I knew I would build a long workbench along one of the garage walls. So I began sketching idea after idea, looking for inspiration in books, magazines, and on TV woodworking shows.

While paging through magazines, I came upon an article for a roll-around tool-storage cabinet designed to be tucked under one wing of a tablesaw. It dawned on me that I could use a similar concept to save space in my garage. Beneath the workbench I could house roll-around cabinets to store tools.

Two Cars and a Workbench

The 23-ft. square space is a workshop by day and a garage by night. A long workbench spanning one wall houses a series of multipurpose rolling cabinets used for storage and as tool stands, work surfaces, and infeed and outfeed tables.

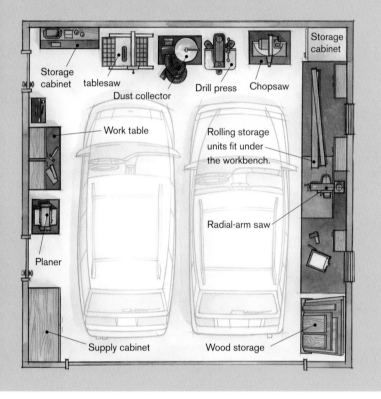

Storage cabinet

tablesaw

Dust collector

Drill press

Chopsaw

Storage cabinet

Storage cabinet

Work table

Rolling storage units fit under the workbench.

Radial-arm saw

Planer

Supply cabinet

Wood storage

The more I thought about it, the more advantages I could see of this system. With the rolling cabinets built to well-planned heights, they could serve as infeed and outfeed supports for the tablesaw, planer, and chopsaw. Work areas also could be adapted to accommodate different projects just by rearranging the rolling cabinets.

Workbench Serves as a Garage for Rolling Cabinets

Constructing the main workbench was the first task. Because of space limitations, I decided to build it in two sections and bolt them together. One section is 8 ft. long, and the other is 6 ft. long. After some

measuring of tables and kitchen cabinets, I determined that a work surface 30 in. deep and 37 in. high would be most comfortable. The workbench was fortified with a 2x4 frame to support the substantial weight of the radial-arm saw. I also installed two electrical-outlet strips on the bench, one on each side of the saw. They're mounted along the front edge to keep power-tool cords from extending across the top of the work surface.

Cabinets Are Built for Mixing and Matching

It was both fun and challenging to design and build the cabinets. Once I knew the workbench measurements, it was easy to back out the dimensions for the rolling cabinets. To keep it simple, the cabinets follow the same basic design but are configured differently, according to their specific functions.

Some cabinets have drawers, some have shelves, and some are built to hold large power tools. All of the cabinets roll on swivel casters. Handles are attached to the cabinet faces so that they can be maneuvered around the garage. The handles, drawer pulls, and cabinet-door handles are all matching brushed chrome, giving the final profile of the workbench a handsome look.

Storage cabinets double as work surfaces The cabinet used for storing power tools has six sliding shelves that pull out to the left for storing sanders, a jigsaw, and other tools. A second cabinet is built in a mirror image with shelves that pull out to the right. Butting these two cabinets together creates a continuous work surface while leaving the shelves accessible.

A third rolling cabinet has five drawers to hold hand tools. A shelf underneath the top of the cabinet is open on three sides, providing a place to set tools and keep them out of the way. The opening also is

Basic Construction of Rolling Cabinets

Each rolling cabinet has the same overall dimensions: 26 in. deep by 22 in. wide by 32½ in. high (the chopsaw, planer, and scrollsaw cabinets are shorter but follow a similar construction method). Locking swivel casters account for 3 in. of the height. The basic construction allows for variations in the placement of drawers and shelves. Each cabinet is constructed from ¾-in.-thick plywood and finished with two coats of water-based varnish.

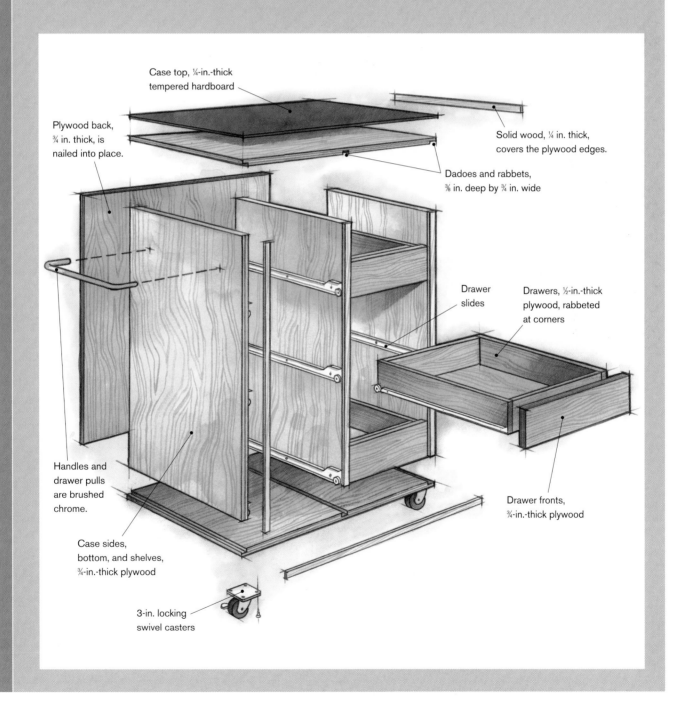

Case top, ¼-in.-thick tempered hardboard

Plywood back, ¾ in. thick, is nailed into place.

Solid wood, ¼ in. thick, covers the plywood edges.

Dadoes and rabbets, ⅜ in. deep by ¾ in. wide

Drawer slides

Drawers, ½-in.-thick plywood, rabbeted at corners

Handles and drawer pulls are brushed chrome.

Drawer fronts, ¾-in.-thick plywood

Case sides, bottom, and shelves, ¾-in.-thick plywood

3-in. locking swivel casters

While confined to set dimensions, Endress designed the rolling cabinets with various arrangements of shelves and drawers so that each one serves a different purpose.

SLIDING SHELVES STORE POWER TOOLS VISIBLY AND WITHIN REACH. Endress built two of these cabinets—one with a left-facing handle, the other with a right-facing handle—to form a large surface when side by side.

SHALLOW DRAWERS HOLD HAND TOOLS. An open area below the top of the cabinet keeps tools within reach but out of the way. The cabinet's top has enough overhang for attaching clamps.

SCROLLSAW SITS AT A COMFORTABLE HEIGHT. The scrollsaw is mounted to this low rolling cabinet so that it can fit below the workbench when not in use. However, it's just the right height to use while sitting comfortably in a chair.

THERE'S NO SUCH THING AS TOO MUCH STORAGE. Two tall, open shelves are used for storing large objects, such as a toolbox, benchtop grinder, and belt sander.

ROUTER TABLE HOLDS PARTS AND ACCESSORIES. This rolling router table is equipped with a router lift. The lift is off-set to accommodate drawers, bits, and accessories. Dust-collection ports are built into the fence and cabinet .

useful for clamping workpieces to the tabletop, as clamp heads can be tightened against the top's overhang.

The fourth cabinet has two shelves accessible from three sides. One shelf holds two toolboxes; the other holds my bench grinder and a small belt sander.

The consistent height of the cabinets makes them ideal as infeed and outfeed tables for my chopsaw, planer, and tablesaw.

Stationary tools get wheels, too The first four cabinets provide adequate storage for my hand tools. But I also needed storage for my assorted power tools.

With the cabinets and tool stands built to corresponding heights, they can be arranged for use in a variety of combinations. The four-station arrangement shown here will accommodate a work flow that includes benchtop planing (1), ripping on the table saw (2), crosscutting on the chopsaw (3), and routing at the router table (4). After an operation has been completed at one station, the outfeed table is rolled to the next station, where it becomes the infeed table.

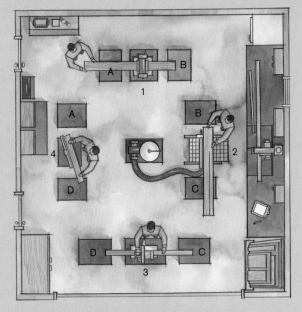

1. ROOM FOR ROUGH CUTTING. Endress starts by milling boards at the thickness planer. Rolling cabinets support the stock on its way in and out of the planer and can be moved for boards of various lengths.

2. SUPPORT FOR LONG OR WIDE STOCK. The planer outfeed table becomes the in-feed support at the tablesaw. A second cabinet catches the board on its way out.

3. INSTANT CHOPSAW STATION. Like the other power tools in this shop, the chopsaw is built on a rolling cabinet designed so that the saw-cutting work surface is level with the tops of the other cabinets.

4. COMFORTABLE ROUTING STATION. After transporting a stack of freshly crosscut material from the chopsaw, Endress goes to work at the router table.

Sources

Woodcraft Supply Corp.

P.O. Box 1686
Parkersburg, WV 26102
800-225-1153
www.woodcraft.com

The scrollsaw fits below the workbench, sitting on a low, rolling cabinet. While it seems quite short at first glance, the cabinet is just the right height for using the saw while you're sitting comfortably in a chair.

The router-table cabinet also is on wheels. The table is equipped with a router lift. The lift is offset from the center of the work surface, leaving room for drawers on one side of the cabinet to hold router bits, collet wrenches, and a laminate trimmer. Two more drawers below the router are large enough to hold another router, associated tools, and auxiliary baseplates.

Following the same design, I built rolling cabinets to hold my planer, chopsaw, and tablesaw. Rather than getting stored out of sight, these cabinets fit along the walls of my shop and can be moved easily. The cabinets for these tools also have plenty of storage for any accessories.

Dust collection is easy to incorporate

The only tool in the shop that doesn't have dust collection built into its cabinet is the chopsaw. Try as I might, I haven't come up with a good dust-collection system that allows me to store the cabinet against the wall. When using this tool, I usually set it up by the garage door so that the dust generated is thrown outside the shop.

To keep the shop clean, I settled on a 1-hp mobile dust collector that can be attached to one tool at a time, and it has been adequate so far.

Wheels roll in any direction and lock

securely I used four 3-in. locking swivel casters (available at hardware stores) on each rolling cabinet, which enables them to move in any direction.

When all four wheels are locked, the cabinet becomes a stable platform. Unfortunately, due primarily to its weight, moving and locking my tablesaw into place on its low cabinet was a struggle. It always seemed to go in the opposite direction I wanted it to go. On a whim, I decided to try higher-quality, heavy-duty casters from Woodcraft Supply Corp. (see "Sources"). What a difference quality makes! Not only can I move my saw with little effort, but the locking mechanism also is much easier to operate.

Wall Cabinets Reduce Clutter

After taking up as much space as I could afford on the ground, I looked to the walls for more storage. I designed the wall cabinets to accommodate my work habits. I did not want deep cabinets, as things tend to get shoved to the back and become lost. I wanted my cabinets just deep enough to hold racks of storage bins. I also did not want them so high that a ladder would be necessary to access the top shelves. This led to a final dimension of 8 in. by 30 in. by 30 in. for a double wide cabinet, and 8 in. by 15 in. by 30 in. for a single wide cabinet.

Cars and Projects Live in Harmony

When I first came up with the idea of a small garage shop based on a mobile storage concept, I wondered how it would work out. After using the shop for more than a year, I continue to be amazed at how easy and how much fun it is to work here. All of my requirements were met, including the ability to park two vehicles in the garage when the shop is not in use.

As with any shop, there are lessons learned for building the next one. In hindsight, it would have been a good idea to plumb the workbench for dust collection and compressed air. But overall I am quite pleased with the current mix of rolling cabinets. If I do add new tools to my shop, I'll build rolling cabinets designed specifically for them.

BILL ENDRESS is an aerospace engineer in Tucson, Arizona. In his spare time, he works wood in his two-car garage.

Versatile Shop
Storage Solutions

THESE MOVABLE CABINETS keep tools stored, on slide-out shelves or in drawers, neat and dust-free. Casters make the base cabinets mobile, while a cleat-mounting system allows the wall cabinets to be easily rearranged.

BY JOSEPH BEALS

During the 10 years I worked in a cellar shop, I installed cabinets, drawers, and open shelving wherever room allowed. The results were typical: I knew where to find everything, but there was little order to the method, and junk and dust were a chronic problem.

When I moved to a converted garage building, I left those built-ins behind. I packed tools, hardware, and supplies into dozens of 5-gal. buckets, and I worked out of them for the next year until the new shop was at last functional. To avoid re-creating the past, I designed a new storage system that remedies many of the usual irritations. I resolved to minimize any sort of generic storage that invites accretions of dust and junk. This meant little or no open shelving, no big drawers under the bench, and no casual boxes or bins.

Finally, with the agony of moving so close behind me, I wanted a fully portable storage system. And I wanted a system that could be moved around easily.

Mobile Cabinets

With these goals in mind, I built a set of floor and wall cabinets, as shown in the photo at left, which offer exceptional utility in concert with a pleasing, traditional appearance; I also built special wall storage racks, as discussed in the box on p. 21. The floor cabinets are mounted on casters and incorporate a series of guide rails for shelves or drawers. The wall cabinets hang from simple wall-mounted cleats (see the photo on p. 22) and include integral dadoes to allow any combination of plain or purpose-built shelving. To cut costs, I built the cabinets from a variety of wood species using leftover stock and cutoffs, including quartersawn white oak, black walnut, mahogany, elm, and cherry. All cabinets include paneled doors, ½-in.-thick birch plywood backs, and straightforward joinery.

Building Considerations

Many woodworkers rely upon detailed, measured drawings as the final design stage, but that's like committing a melody to manuscript without opening the piano for a trial run. Unless you have an extraordinary ability to assess light and shadow, mass, proportion, and function on paper, you risk building a sterile, technocratic piece. Remember that a final measured drawing merely records the component dimensions of a functional, aesthetically pleasing prototype.

I used molded frames, raised panels, and polished finish to create a display for clients visiting my shop, but there are many simpler options. Pine frames made on the tablesaw, router table, or entirely by hand, together with ¼-in.-thick plywood panels and a paint finish, are attractive and require no special tooling. A solid, flat panel, rabbeted around the perimeter to fit the frame grooves, is fully traditional and easy to make. If you are new to frame-and-panel work, these alternatives are a practical and satisfying introduction.

For a contemporary appearance, substitute plywood for frame-and-panel construction. Plywood cabinet sides can be grooved to house shelving or drawers, eliminating the guide rails required by a frame-and-panel carcase. Plywood has some drawbacks, however. A-C fir plywood is generally too crude for cabinetry, but ¾-in.-thick birch plywood, which is the least expensive alternative, will cost about $45* per sheet and is best suited for a paint finish. Also, exposed plywood edges must be banded for a good appearance, even under paint. Commercial banding veneers with a hot-melt adhesive are easy to apply, but shopmade solid edge-banding is more robust, and it looks better.

Base Cabinets

I built all the cabinets in multiples for maximum benefit of bench and machine time, but I'll describe the construction as if I were making only one of each, starting with a floor cabinet. I began with the frame-and-panel sides (see figure 1 on facing page). The stiles are equal in length to the height of the frame, but stile and rail widths and the length of the rails are determined according to personal preference and the method of joinery. Mortise-and-tenon joinery, for example, requires additional length on the rails for the tenons.

I used a matched set of cope-and-pattern cutters on the shaper to machine the frame, but there are many other equally suitable methods. To ensure accuracy, I took panel dimensions off a dry-assembled frame. After preparing the stock, I wasted the bulk of the bevel on the tablesaw, and then finished fielding the panel with a panel-raising cutter on the shaper.

When the two sides were assembled and cleaned up, I used my shaper to cut a rabbet on the inside back edge to receive the plywood back and another across the inside top edge to house the upper web frame. Finally, I installed the maple drawer and shelf guides. The guide spacing is uniform, so any drawer will fit any space. And drawers and shelves are interchangeable, as shown in the bottom photo on p. 23. To

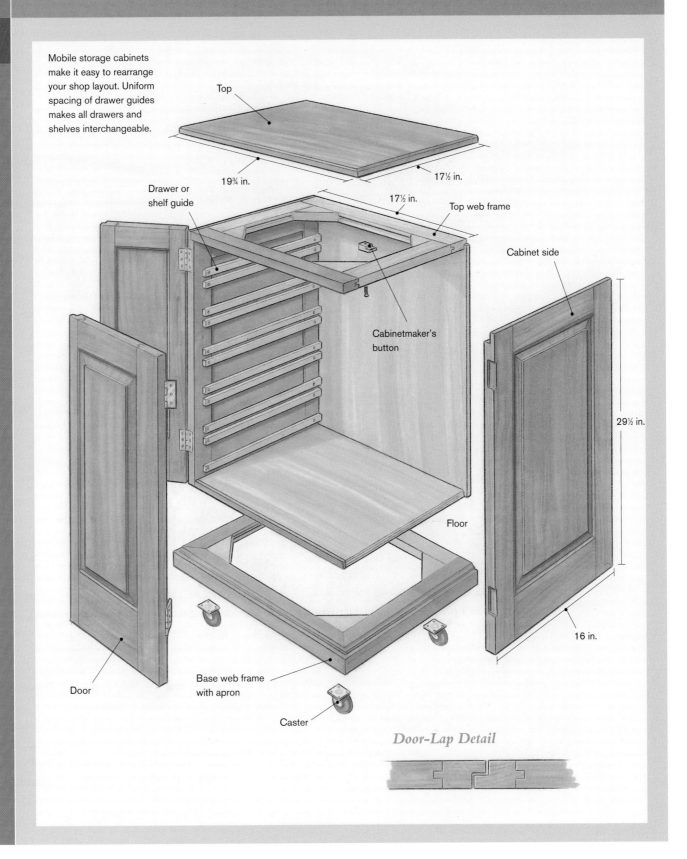

Mobile storage cabinets make it easy to rearrange your shop layout. Uniform spacing of drawer guides makes all drawers and shelves interchangeable.

Top

19¾ in.

17½ in.

Drawer or shelf guide

17½ in.

Top web frame

Cabinet side

Cabinetmaker's button

29½ in.

Floor

Door

Base web frame with apron

Caster

16 in.

Door-Lap Detail

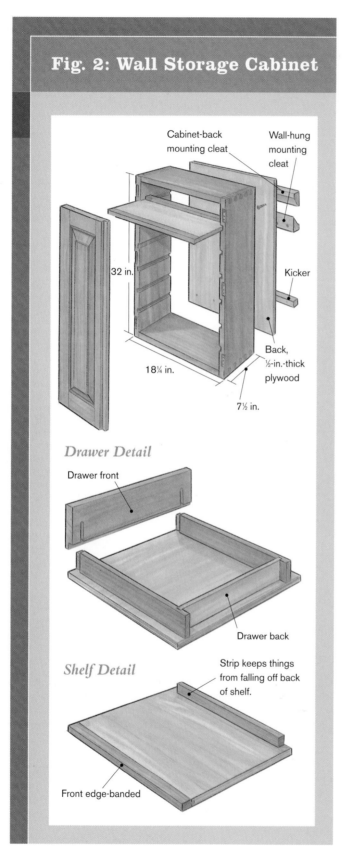

Fig. 2: Wall Storage Cabinet

Cabinet-back mounting cleat

Wall-hung mounting cleat

32 in.

Kicker

18¼ in.

Back, ½-in.-thick plywood

7½ in.

Drawer Detail

Drawer front

Drawer back

Shelf Detail

Strip keeps things from falling off back of shelf.

Front edge-banded

make this job accurate and quick, the guides are prepared in advance with counterbored screw holes and positioned with a series of spacers, as shown in the top photo on p. 23. That ensures consistent, square placement. I load the screws into their holes and run them in with production-line speed.

An upper web frame keeps the top of the carcase square, and provides fastening for the solid top and an upper stop for the doors. Notice that the front member of the web is full length and is the only part that needs to be primary wood. For a run of several cabinets, using secondary wood for the sides, back and corner blocks can save an appreciable amount of stock. A lower web frame is the load-bearing part of the cabinet base. The lower web is exposed on the front and both sides with the two front joints mitered for a better appearance.

Both web frames are of traditional construction, as shown in figure 1. I used a shaper to machine the full-length grooves, and I cut the tongues on the tablesaw. I also splined the lower web miter joints for strength and convenience of positioning during assembly. To avoid juggling eight parts at once, I first glued the web frames without corner blocks. When the glue has set, the corner blocks are installed in a second operation.

A skirt on the front and sides of the lower web frame gives visual mass to the cabinet base and shrouds the casters. After the skirt was applied, I used a pair of cutters on the shaper to machine a simple reverse ogee (cyma reversa) molding detail on the front and sides, giving a graceful transition from the carcase to the base. Finally, a plywood shelf is affixed to the top of the lower web frame, with the front edge-banded with the cabinet's primary wood. The shelf provides a cabinet floor and positive positioning for the cabinet sides, and the front edge serves as a lower door stop.

Wall Racks for Clamps, Lumber, or Shelves

With tools and hardware stowed out of sight in the new cabinetry, I was still left with a pile of clamps along one wall and a stack of lumber on the floor. My solution to both problems was the same, as shown in the photo below and the drawing at right. The lumber rack is identical to the pipe-clamp rack but built with more substantial members.

The racks are built by sandwiching spacer blocks between two vertical pieces to create mortises that hold the support arms. The support arms are angled on their lower edges, and the wedges that hold the arms in place have a matching angle on their upper edges. To secure the support arm, slip it into the mortise, push the wedge into the mortise below the arm and tap the wedge into place with a hammer. The arms can hold clamps, lumber, or even shelves for storing other small items.

WALL RACKS FOR CLAMPS and lumber storage are easily made by sandwiching spacer blocks between a pair of vertical supports. Support arms slide into mortises and are secured with a wedge.

WALL RACKS

Simply constructed, this rack can hold lumber, pipe clamps or even shelves. Use 2x stock for the lumber rack; smaller stock is sufficient for other purposes.

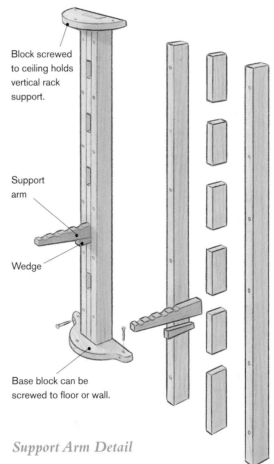

Block screwed to ceiling holds vertical rack support.

Support arm

Wedge

Base block can be screwed to floor or wall.

Support Arm Detail

To make detents that prevent pipes from rolling off support arms, drill 1-in.-dia. holes after clamping the support arms together, top edge to top edge, separated by a ½-in.-wide spacer.

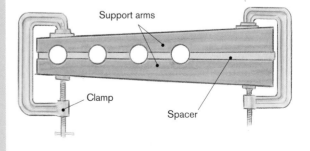

Support arms

Clamp

Spacer

All the cabinet components are screwed together, so assembling the cabinet is quick and easy. The two sides are fastened to the lower web frame with screws driven up from below, just inside the skirt. The upper web frame is screwed down into the sides from the top and the plywood back is screwed into the rabbets that house it. I used no glue in the assembly, which makes it possible to take the carcase apart for any reason. I used shop-grade elm for a serviceable top on all floor cabinets. The tops are given a half-round profile on the front and sides, and they're fastened to the upper web frame with traditional buttons (see figure 1 on p. 19).

The cabinet shelves can be solid stock or sheet goods, as preference dictates. I used ½-in.-thick birch plywood, banded on the front to match the cabinet wood. The shelves pull out easily on the guides, and thin cleats glued to the back keep things from falling off the back edge.

To keep the design simple, I built the drawers as a box fastened to a shelf, as shown in the detail on p. 20. The two sides engage the front with sliding dovetail joints, and the front of the shelf fits in a rabbet on the drawer front. I screwed the sides and back to the bottom from below. The cabinet will hold six shallow drawers, but deeper drawers can be made by doubling or tripling the spacing module.

Building Wall Cabinets

Construction of the wall cabinets is simplicity itself (see figure 2 on p. 20). The solid carcase can be assembled in a variety of ways, but through-dovetails offer the strongest and best-looking joint. I cut all dovetails by hand, which took less than an hour for each cabinet. Before the carcase was assembled, I used a dado set on the radial-arm saw to cut six shelf dadoes in each side. Using steel shelf standards or a series of holes for shelf-support pins would provide a greater range of spacing options

CLEATS ALLOW CABINETS TO BE MOVED. Strips ripped at 45 degrees, one screwed to the wall and one to the cabinet back, make it easy to rearrange cabinets. A kicker screwed to the cabinet back near the bottom makes the cabinet hang plumb.

and a cleaner look, but my prior experience with these methods was unsatisfactory. A fully housed shelf never tips out nor does it require a store of mounting pins or brackets, which are typically missing at the moment of need.

Finally, I machined a rabbet on the inside back edges to house the plywood back. The rabbet is full length on top and bottom and is stopped ¼ in. short of the ends on each side. I cut the rabbets on the shaper and cleaned the stopped ends with a chisel after the carcase was assembled. The back rabbet could also be routed with a bearing-guided bit or on a tablesaw. When the back is in place, a hanging cleat is fastened near the top (see the photo above), and a kicker is fitted near the bottom to keep the hung cabinet vertical.

INSTALLING DRAWER GUIDES is done with production-line speed by drilling counterbored screw holes and positioning the guides with spacers.

DRAWERS AND SHELVING ARE INTERCHANGEABLE because the guide spacing is uniform. Salvaged stock was used for the veneered drawer fronts.

Frame-and-Panel Doors

All cabinets are provided with a pair of narrow, paneled doors. A single-wide door might seem simpler, but the sweep can be awkward, especially on a floor cabinet in a restricted space. The doors are constructed like the floor cabinet sides and for appearance have the same dimensional proportions of stiles and rails. Notice, however, that the two inside stiles are half-width and give the appearance of a single, full-width stile when the doors are closed. The stiles are also half-lapped, as shown in the door-lap detail on p. 19, such that a single catch on the right-hand door keeps both doors closed. I cut the inside stiles wide to assemble the doors and machined the lap joint after assembly.

I used aniline dye to stain all but the cherry cabinet. Because cherry darkens so rapidly and dramatically, it is generally better not to color the wood under the finish. All cabinets received a half dozen coats of shellac, and after the last coat was well rubbed out, I applied a beeswax polish for a soft, lustrous finish.

★Please note that price estimates are from 1994.

JOSEPH BEALS is a builder and custom wood-worker who lives in Marshfield, Massachusetts.

ELEGANT CABINETS

Four Ways to Get Organized

W oodworkers who are passionate about their craft spend a lot of time in their shops, perhaps more than in any other room of their homes. It's no surprise, then, that many woodworkers go out of their way to set up a comfortable, organized, even elegant workspace. You can tell from the way these craftsmen have set up their shops that they take great pride in their work. Following are snapshots from four shops scattered coast to coast that show the creativity of their owners. We hope they inspire you to make your shop a better place to work.

MOVABLE TOOL RACKS

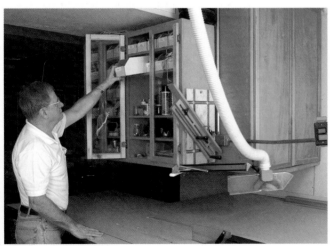

USING WASTED SPACE

REVOLVING TOOL RACK

Elegant Cabinets
BY DAVE PADGET

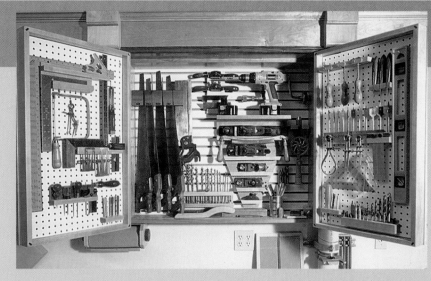

Tool storage chests and cabinets are an ancient and respected art form worthy of our best efforts. Besides their obvious usefulness, well-designed toolboxes allow craftsmen to test and demonstrate their skills. I can't help but think that these works also provide their makers with great satisfaction and enjoyment.

I know that shops are usually works in progress, constantly evolving to meet new requirements. Therefore, when designing my present shop, I tried to make things adjustable, convertible, or adaptable to mitigate the scarring of the shop that inevitably results from perpetual changes. However, I still wanted the workbench and tool cabinets to be permanent fixtures and placed them along a wall, freeing up the center of the shop for my table saw.

The 10-in.-deep by 144-in.-wide by 45-in.-high tool cabinet over the work-

bench is, without a doubt, the focal point of the shop. It features six maple raised frame-and-panel doors with walnut splined corners. The case is topped with a high crown cornice with two maple crown moldings accented with black walnut trim. The fluted pilasters separating the three sections of the cabinet have corbels at the top supporting the cornice. A small pullout shelf at the bottom of each pilaster keeps my coffee cup off the workbench. One

T-SLOTTED PANELS, COMMON IN RETAIL DISPLAYS, ARE USED INSIDE THE CABINETS. Custom-made tool holders fit into the slots. The backs of the doors are fitted with pegboard.

of the pilasters houses a 4-in. dust-collection duct.

Inside the cabinet my tools are hung on T-slotted panels (commonly seen in retail displays). These panels are for mounting fixtures and require a metal bracket that slips into the slot. They are durable, stable, and easily adapted to a variety of needs. The panels and the metal brackets can be ordered from commercial retail merchandising distributors such as Too Home (see www.toohome.com).

A workbench often is called upon to handle tasks other than woodworking. Tools such as lawn mowers and chainsaws aren't kind to a maple benchtop. That's why I covered 5 ft. of my 12-ft.-long bench with a stainless-steel cap.

The woodworking section of my bench is laminated maple with a maple face and end vises with walnut handles and walnut benchdogs. There is also a bench slave on the right leg to support long material in the face vise. The

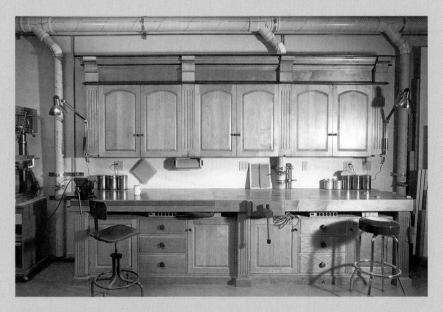

SOLID-WOOD CABINETS DRESS UP THE SHOP. Padget loves spending time in his shop, and he's made it as elegant as the rest of his home.

Elegant Cabinets (continued)
BY DAVE PADGET

SWIVELING VERTICAL STORAGE UNIT. One edge is fastened to the wall with heavy hinges, and casters underneath allow the unit to pivot for easy access.

bench features raised frame-and-panel ends and fluted pilaster legs. A maple storage cabinet under the work surface houses drawers with black walnut sides dovetailed to maple faces and sliding maple tills with walnut splined corners. The bench also is equipped with 110-volt and 220-volt power, high-pressure air, and a vacuum.

Elsewhere in the shop I have two rolling storage units (one vertical, one horizontal) for sheet goods. These units have heavy-duty hinges on one side attached to the wall or adjoining cabinet. Two 3-in. heavy-duty casters on the other end support the outward end off the floor and allow the unit to be swung or rolled out from the wall for easy access to the contents. It can be pushed back against the wall and out of the way. One of the rolling units can be made from a 12-ft. 2x10 and one 4x8 sheet of plywood. I mounted the vertical unit on the side of the clamp storage closet. The horizontal unit is mounted to a wall shelf support. All of the shelving in my shop is attached to the walls rather than standing on the floor (saving precious floor space) and is totally adjustable.

The pursuit of shop storage perfection will go on and on because it is as individualized as each woodworker. The important thing is to engage in and enjoy the creative process.

DAVE PADGET works wood in Olympia, Washington.

Movable Tool Racks
BY CARL SWENSSON

I work in a cinder-block basement shop and, needless to say, the walls are not pretty. I've partly solved this problem and answered the question of how to store most of my hand tools by building simple tool racks out of clear pine. The racks lend a warm touch to an otherwise visually cold working environment.

The racks are hung on French cleats, which allow me to move a whole set of tools to where I'm working in the shop. I went a little overboard by gluing up blocking to the front of the cleats (and to the front of the lower spacer blocks as well) to create breadboard ends. The blocking extends just a hair beyond the face of the rack and produces a shadow line, which lends a finished look.

This simple tool-rack design is practical for many reasons. First, I know where every tool is at a glance. Because the most-used tools are so easily and conveniently stored, I'm less apt to let them pile up and clutter my bench when working.

To add or subtract tools from the racks, all I need is a claw hammer and a fistful of nails. Although you can hang a

IT'S EASY TO RECONFIGURE A TOOL RACK. Just pull out the nails and start over.

WALL-HUNG, SOLID-WOOD RACKS are not only adaptable but also cover cinder blocks.

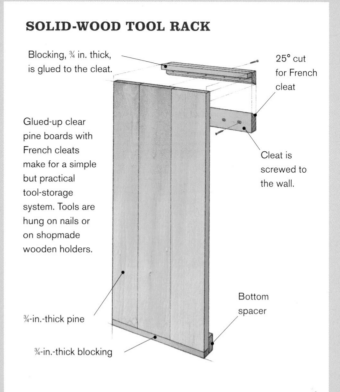

SOLID-WOOD TOOL RACK

Blocking, ¾ in. thick, is glued to the cleat.

25° cut for French cleat

Glued-up clear pine boards with French cleats make for a simple but practical tool-storage system. Tools are hung on nails or on shopmade wooden holders.

Cleat is screwed to the wall.

¾-in.-thick pine

Bottom spacer

¾-in.-thick blocking

lot of tools just by a nail alone, I did make a number of wooden holders for things like chisels and hammers. Most of these holders are simple blocks of wood with notched holes that allow a tool to be slipped into and out of the holder without being raised very far and bumping into tools above. If you design your holders so that tools must be lifted up and out, you have to leave room above, which wastes space.

Last, I've noticed that when my customers visit my shop, they enjoy seeing this orderly display of tools. It gives them a sense of what is needed to create a piece of furniture.

CARL SWENSSON designs furniture and teaches woodworking in Baltimore, Maryland.

SWENSSON USES CLEAR PINE BOARDS FOR TOOL RACKS. The pine is a warm, pleasant alternative to the drab, cinder-block walls of his shop.

Using Wasted Space

BY FRED SOTCHER

A well-designed storage system makes it easy to find tools and hardware, allows for flexibility as needs change, and makes the best use of limited space. It also should be low in cost, look good, and show off the more attractive tools. I have a variety of storage systems in my basement shop that meet these requirements.

I've never seen storage cabinets that hang out over part of the tablesaw. But that's exactly what I built. My cabinets fill the wasted space to the right and rear of the blade and store jigs for the saw. Doors on both ends let in enough light for me to find things easily. The cabinets are set far enough out of the way that I never run into a problem when cutting tenons or other tall parts.

You hardly ever see glass-faced cabinets in workshops, but I built some anyway. In the 13 years since, I have yet to break one pane of glass. I did mount them rather high, at about the same level you would install kitchen cabinets. I can spot what I need from halfway across the room.

If you have a set of stairs leading into your shop, build shelves or pullout drawers to fit under the treads. You'd be surprised at how much stuff can be put away in this awkward space.

There are a lot of small items that need to be stored in the average workshop, including screws, hinges, template rings for routers, and replacement parts. Instead of tossing them in drawers or on shelves where they will get mixed up, I use jars, plastic storage bins, and what are known as stock boxes, cardboard storage bins that you can buy from industrial suppliers such as Grainger™ and MSC (www.grainger.com and www.mscdirect.com).

I like to have my hand and power tools within easy reach. For them, I built angled (set at 15 degrees) display racks. I screwed French cleats to the faces of the racks to hang specially designed tool holders. Heavy tools have dedicated holders. This system allows me to reconfigure the racks as needed.

FRED SOTCHER is a retired electrical engineer who works wood in San Jose, California.

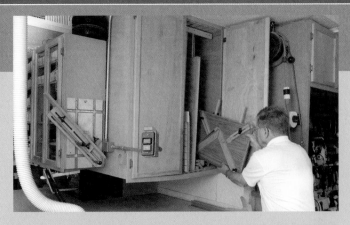

OVERHEAD CABINETS RESIDE ABOVE THE TABLESAW. Sotcher likes glass-door panels (left in photo) because they make it a lot easier to locate tools. And he says he has not broken one pane in 13 years.

ADJUSTABLE WOOD STORAGE RACK. The rack is converted from horizontal storage to vertical storage by simply removing the crosspieces.

ANGLED TOOL RACKS ARE PLACED ABOVE THE BENCH. Individual tool holders are attached to the rack with French cleats.

Revolving Tool Rack

BY JOE JOHNS

Whether your shop is large or small, and your tool collection miserly or princely, it is satisfying to figure out storage solutions that are efficient, adaptable, and inexpensive. Now, I don't have anything against pegboard, but frankly, pegboard is boring. I like to show off my creativity in the shop as well as in my woodworking. That's why I designed a swiveling tool rack.

My tool rack makes highly efficient use of wall space. It takes up only about 15 sq. ft. but returns 40 sq. ft. of storage (both sides of the panels are usable). The panels don't bump into each other because they're all linked via sprockets by a length of chain.

The construction of the panels couldn't be simpler. They consist of ½-in.-thick medium-density overlay (MDO, which is fir plywood covered with paper), surrounded by a 2-in.-thick frame of medium-density fiberboard (MDF). Each panel is centered on a metal pin attached to a sprocket connected to a length of chain. A second pin is attached to the top of each panel frame. I fitted my panels between upper and lower cabinets (the pins on the frames fit into matching holes in the cabinets). But to simplify things, you could fit the panels between a pair of L-shaped plywood support brackets bolted to the wall. Be sure to use lag bolts and tap into the studs. For tool holders, I drilled holes in the panels to accept lengths of wooden dowels and steel rods. It's easiest to do this with the tools arranged on a panel laid flat.

JOE JOHNS lives in Ronan, Montana, where he specializes in furniture design, antique repair and refinishing, and custom cabinetry.

FIVE-PANEL TOOL RACK REVOLVES. Johns's tool rack provides about 40 sq. ft. of storage while taking up only 15 sq. ft. of wall space.

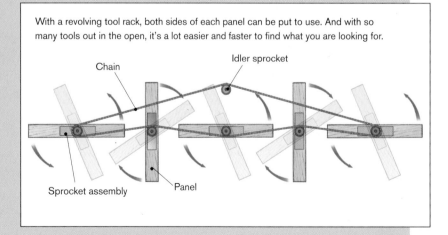

With a revolving tool rack, both sides of each panel can be put to use. And with so many tools out in the open, it's a lot easier and faster to find what you are looking for.

Chain

Idler sprocket

Sprocket assembly

Panel

Clamp Storage Solutions

THE WALL OF A LUMBER RACK doubles as a place to store clamps.

Clamps are to woodshops what closets are to houses: You can't have too many of them.

Band clamps, bar clamps, C–clamps, corner clamps, edge clamps, hand clamps, miter clamps, pipe clamps, quick clamps, spring clamps. Each style of clamp is useful for a particular purpose, but storing them all, with their different shapes and lengths, can be a challenge. You can pile them all in a corner or throw them into a drawer. Or you can organize them on a wall or a movable cart that will make them easy to get at when you need them and will keep them out of the way when you don't. What follows are examples of how some woodworkers solved their clamp-storage problems.

Having recently moved to a smaller shop, I had to find somewhere to store my fairly large collection of bar clamps and hand clamps. When considering where to put them, I decided against a fancy rack that rolls around the shop on casters because the floor space it would require is too dear. I wanted my clamps near the area where large glue-up projects will be done, but I also wanted to keep them out of the way when they're not needed. The solution was to hang the clamps on the outside wall of a lumber-storage rack.

The racks I designed are quite simple, and they can be used to store a variety of different-size clamps. First, securely fasten a ¾-in.-thick hanger strip (plywood or medium-density fiberboard) to the wall, using two screws at every stud location. This hanger strip serves two purposes: It's a sturdy anchor, and it adds depth for building out the rack enough to make a good ledge on which to hang the bar clamps. Along the bottom of the hanger strip goes another ¾-in. plywood cleat (what some people call a French cleat) with a 45 degree cut along the top edge. That bottom cleat gets screwed to the hanger cleat. Another matching plywood cleat with a 45 degree cut along the bottom edge has blocks of lumber screwed into the front face from behind; these blocks are spaced apart so there's room to hang the clamps on them. Nothing fancy—most of the racks I used were salvaged from my previous shop, where they'd given 22 years of faithful service. Depending on the type of clamps, they will hang better facing in or out, because of how the weight is balanced. On the 12-ft. wall shown on the facing page, I currently store 108 clamps, and there's room for more.

JOHN WEST owns and operates Cope and Mould Millwork in Ridgefield, Connecticut.

BAR-CLAMP RACK

By hanging all of his clamps on one wall, West can space the hanging racks apart as necessary to fit different sizes of clamps. The deep-throat bar clamps face outward; the more traditional, older-style bar clamps face the wall. This rack was made longer to allow room for a growing collection of clamps.

MOUNTING DETAIL

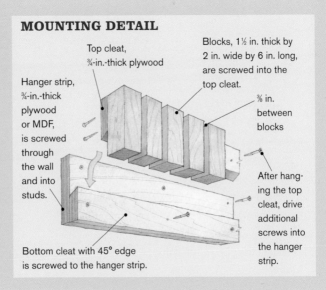

Top cleat, ¾-in.-thick plywood

Blocks, 1½ in. thick by 2 in. wide by 6 in. long, are screwed into the top cleat.

Hanger strip, ¾-in.-thick plywood or MDF, is screwed through the wall and into studs.

⅜ in. between blocks

After hanging the top cleat, drive additional screws into the hanger strip.

Bottom cleat with 45° edge is screwed to the hanger strip.

Ceiling and Wall Racks

BY BROOK DUERR

In my basement shop, wall space and open floor space are scarce. Faced with a growing collection of all kinds of clamps, I didn't know where to store them. One day it dawned on me that I could make use of the unfinished ceiling, with its exposed joists, and one wall alcove to store clamps out of the way. I designed and built several different racks, basing the design on the dimensions of each type of clamp.

For my bar clamps, I constructed each rack with two strips of ¾-in.-thick Baltic birch plywood, fastened together into a T shape with screws driven through the top plate. The top plate is 1½ in. wide, and the vertical piece is 3 in. wide; the lengths will vary according to the number of clamps of each size you need to store. Before assembling the two pieces, I used a dado blade to cut a series of ½-in. by 1½-in. dadoes to serve as slots for slipping the clamps into the racks. You could use a finger-joint jig on the tablesaw if you have a lot of dadoes to cut, but I simply marked each one with a pencil line. To fasten the racks to the underside of the joists, I used a pocket-screw jig, alternating every other screw from one side of the rack to the other. Then I put the clamps into the closed position and slipped them into the racks with the bottom end first.

For all of my Quick-Grip clamps, I made a rack out of a single piece of plywood, ¾ in. thick by 5 in. wide. The plywood is screwed into a joist from below. I cut a series of dadoes on one side only for hanging each clamp. I also used the dado blade to cut a groove in the top surface that runs the length of that edge. The rivets on the bottoms of the clamps sit in that groove and keep the clamps from falling out.

BAR-CLAMP CEILING RACK

To hold bar clamps, Duerr fastened plywood racks directly to the underside of the ceiling joists. He staggered the position of the racks to accommodate various lengths of bar clamps.

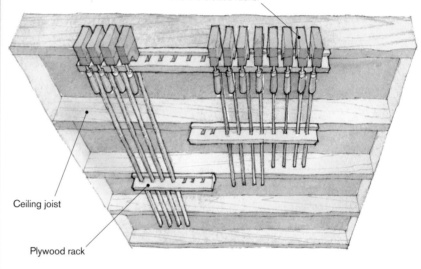

Close clamp heads before inserting clamps into the slotted racks.

Ceiling joist

Plywood rack

MOUNTING DETAIL

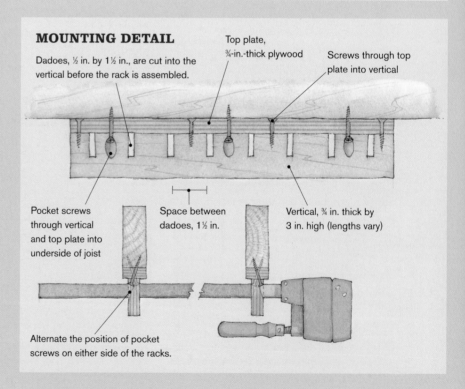

Dadoes, ½ in. by 1½ in., are cut into the vertical before the rack is assembled.

Top plate, ¾-in.-thick plywood

Screws through top plate into vertical

Pocket screws through vertical and top plate into underside of joist

Space between dadoes, 1½ in.

Vertical, ¾ in. thick by 3 in. high (lengths vary)

Alternate the position of pocket screws on either side of the racks.

QUICK-CLAMP CEILING RACK

After running out of room on a wall rack, Duerr added this ceiling rack. He routed a groove into the top to stabilize the hanging clamps and keep them from falling out.

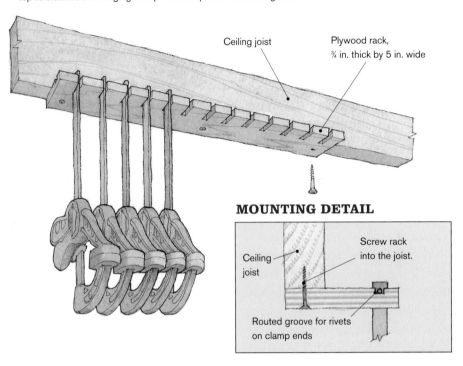

Ceiling joist

Plywood rack, ¾ in. thick by 5 in. wide

MOUNTING DETAIL

Ceiling joist

Screw rack into the joist.

Routed groove for rivets on clamp ends

For my pipe clamps I arrived at a solution similar to the ceiling racks for my bar clamps. I drilled a series of 1½-in.-dia. holes in matching pairs of ¾-in.-thick material and mounted them onto a plywood back, which in turn was screwed to studs against a wall where I store my dust collector. I drilled the holes 3½ in. apart, but if I had to do it again, I'd make the spacing about 5 in. apart for more clearance of the clamp heads. With this design, it's important that one end is on the outside corner of the wall so that the clamp handles don't bind against the wall as you place the pipe clamps into the rack; then you'll have easy access to them when you need them.

BROOK DUERR is a research scientist for a medical-device manufacturer. He does woodworking in his basement shop in a suburb of St. Paul, Minnesota.

PIPE-CLAMP WALL RACK

A small alcove near a dust collector became a perfect spot to install this rack.

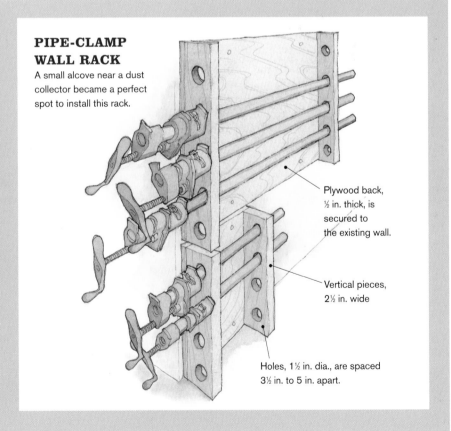

Plywood back, ½ in. thick, is secured to the existing wall.

Vertical pieces, 2½ in. wide

Holes, 1½ in. dia., are spaced 3½ in. to 5 in. apart.

Clamp Cart

BY DAVID DIRANNA

I took up woodworking 24 years ago when I received a radial-arm saw as a present. For most of that time, I had to share shop space with two cars in a three-car garage. But about five years ago, I kicked out the cars, reorganized the layout of the shop, and built storage cabinets along many of the walls.

The end result gave me a lot more floor space to work in, and so when the time came to figure out how to store my small clamp collection, I decided a mobile cart was the best solution for me. I put most of the machinery on casters for the same reason—I like the freedom of being able to move things around. On one end, two casters are fixed, while the other two are swivel—that combination works best.

My main problem with clamps is that I keep buying more. When I first started building this clamp-storage cart, I didn't have a master design for it as it now looks, because I had many fewer clamps than I do now. The design of the cart has undergone a sort of organic evolutionary process.

The purchase of every new batch of clamps has turned this into a modular construction project. I just keep finding ways to add onto the cart to accommodate my most recent clamp purchases. The cart got so heavy at one point that I found it necessary to replace the original 3-in. casters with a heavier-duty 5-in. ball-bearing style. I figured out recently that I'm storing more than $2,000 worth of clamps on the cart. I just hope I don't find it necessary to buy any more.

DAVID DIRANNA taught college-level business courses for many years before switching careers to a business-management position.

HAVE CLAMPS, WILL TRAVEL. Blessed with plenty of floor space, DiRanna chose to put all of his many clamps on a rolling cart.

CLAMP CART

When floor space is plentiful, rolling storage racks bring the clamps to where you need them.

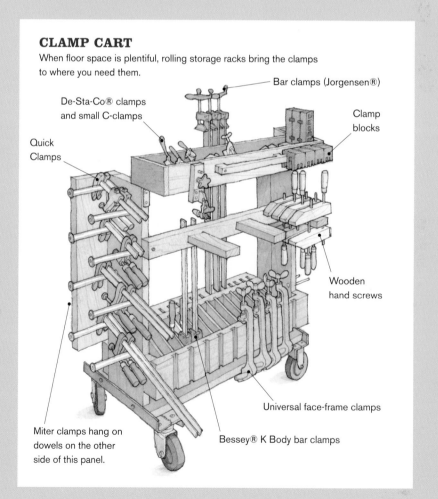

Bar clamps (Jorgensen®)

De-Sta-Co® clamps and small C-clamps

Clamp blocks

Quick Clamps

Wooden hand screws

Miter clamps hang on dowels on the other side of this panel.

Universal face-frame clamps

Bessey® K Body bar clamps

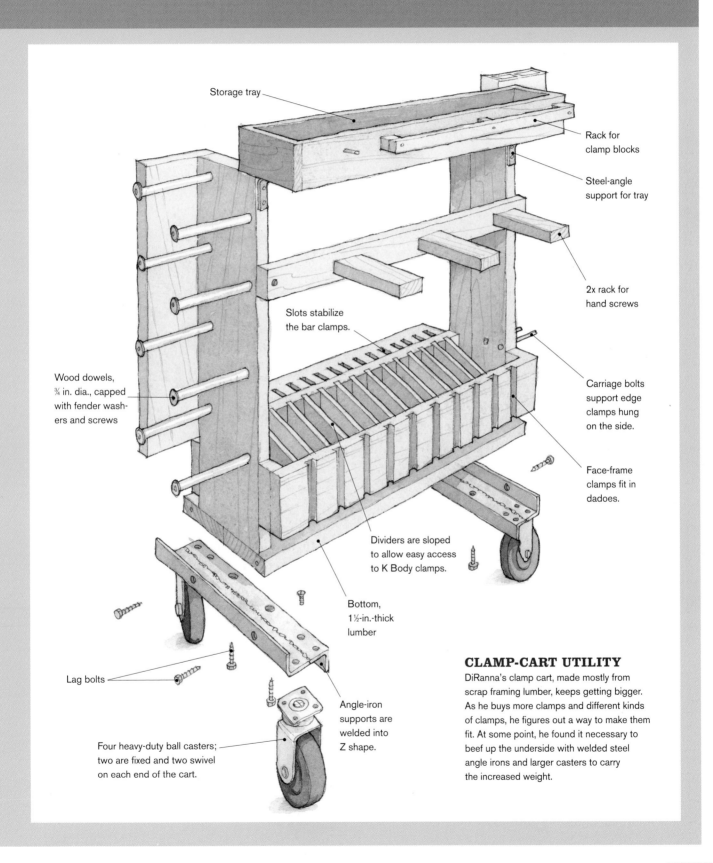

Storage tray

Rack for
clamp blocks

Steel-angle
support for tray

2x rack for
hand screws

Slots stabilize
the bar clamps.

Wood dowels,
¾ in. dia., capped
with fender wash-
ers and screws

Carriage bolts
support edge
clamps hung
on the side.

Face-frame
clamps fit in
dadoes.

Dividers are sloped
to allow easy access
to K Body clamps.

Bottom,
1½-in.-thick
lumber

Lag bolts

Angle-iron
supports are
welded into
Z shape.

Four heavy-duty ball casters;
two are fixed and two swivel
on each end of the cart.

CLAMP-CART UTILITY

DiRanna's clamp cart, made mostly from
scrap framing lumber, keeps getting bigger.
As he buys more clamps and different kinds
of clamps, he figures out a way to make them
fit. At some point, he found it necessary to
beef up the underside with welded steel
angle irons and larger casters to carry
the increased weight.

Tilt-Top
Shop Cart

BY FRED SOTCHER

The first time I manhandled a sheet of 1-in.-thick medium-density fiberboard (MDF) onto my tablesaw, I realized that I needed something to assist with this backbreaking task. So I set out to design a materials-handling cart. But I wanted more than just a plywood mover. My wish list required this shop aid to do the following tasks:

1. Assist with feeding large boards and sheet goods onto the tablesaw
2. Transport sheet goods and other materials from my truck to the shop
3. Double as an additional bench surface when needed
4. Act as a tablesaw infeed/outfeed table
5. Store conveniently out of the way

It's safe to say that the cart I created meets all of those requirements. The tilting top makes it easy to load and feed sheet goods onto the tablesaw. Heavy-duty casters allow me to wheel it around the shop easily. And it also works as an independent bench or as an outfeed table extension to my tablesaw.

I wanted a top that remained flat yet was light in weight, so I chose torsion-box construction. The interior is made up of 3-in.-wide pine strips stapled and glued into 5-in. squares. The box then is framed with a thicker hardwood and the two sides are covered with Masonite®. Pressure laminate is applied over the Masonite on the top. Two ⅛-in. by 12-in. by 12-in. metal angles (Simpson 1212L), with one leg cut off each at 7 in., support the shelf, which is constructed of hardwood.

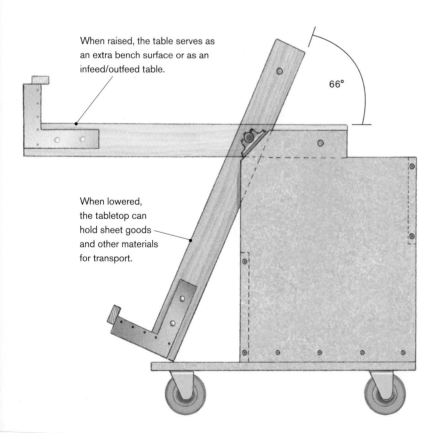

When raised, the table serves as an extra bench surface or as an infeed/outfeed table.

66°

When lowered, the tabletop can hold sheet goods and other materials for transport.

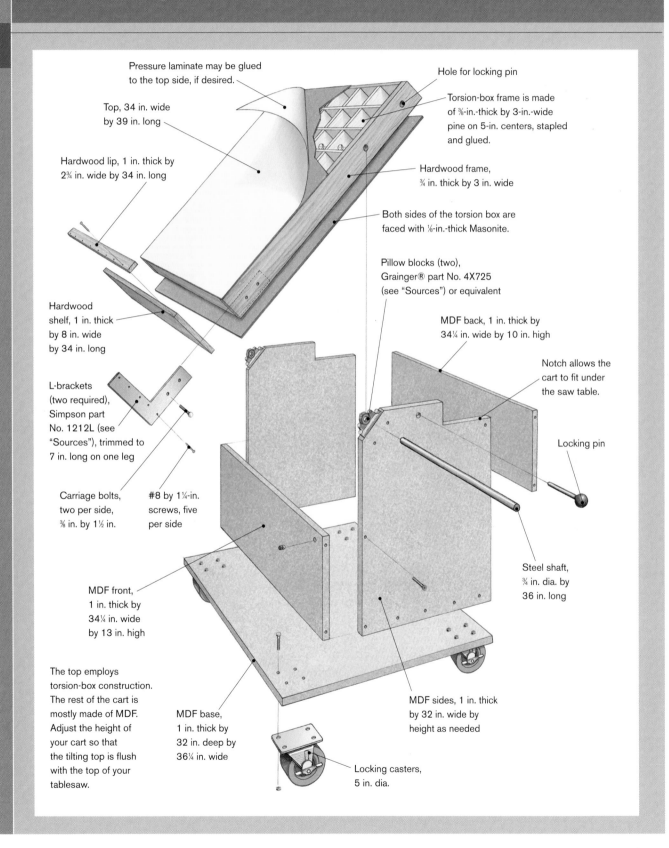

Pressure laminate may be glued to the top side, if desired.

Top, 34 in. wide by 39 in. long

Hardwood lip, 1 in. thick by 2¾ in. wide by 34 in. long

Hardwood shelf, 1 in. thick by 8 in. wide by 34 in. long

L-brackets (two required), Simpson part No. 1212L (see "Sources"), trimmed to 7 in. long on one leg

Carriage bolts, two per side, ⅜ in. by 1½ in.

#8 by 1¼-in. screws, five per side

MDF front, 1 in. thick by 34¼ in. wide by 13 in. high

The top employs torsion-box construction. The rest of the cart is mostly made of MDF. Adjust the height of your cart so that the tilting top is flush with the top of your tablesaw.

MDF base, 1 in. thick by 32 in. deep by 36¼ in. wide

Hole for locking pin

Torsion-box frame is made of ⅜-in.-thick by 3-in.-wide pine on 5-in. centers, stapled and glued.

Hardwood frame, ¾ in. thick by 3 in. wide

Both sides of the torsion box are faced with ⅛-in.-thick Masonite.

Pillow blocks (two), Grainger® part No. 4X725 (see "Sources") or equivalent

MDF back, 1 in. thick by 34¼ in. wide by 10 in. high

Notch allows the cart to fit under the saw table.

Locking pin

Steel shaft, ¾ in. dia. by 36 in. long

MDF sides, 1 in. thick by 32 in. wide by height as needed

Locking casters, 5 in. dia.

The L-Shaped Tilting Top Holds Several Sheets of Plywood

A PIN LOCKS THE TABLETOP IN THE HORIZONTAL POSITION. **Large locking casters can handle bumps in the concrete without stalling. Pillow blocks make for a smooth pivoting action.**

Sources

www.grainger.com
www.strongtie.co.uk
(Simpson Strong-Tie)

The base of the cart is built using 1-in.-thick MDF and connected with 1/4-20 knockdown fasteners. (You could probably get by with ¾-in.-thick MDF.) A ¾-in.-dia. shaft extends through the table and terminates in pillow blocks at both ends, forming the pivot point for the table. With the pivot point near the center of gravity of the sheet goods, you can pivot several hundred pounds of material with little effort. At the opposite end of the table, a ⅜-in.-dia. locking pin is used to lock the top in the horizontal position.

I made the cart the same height as my tablesaw. When I'm not using it to feed stock, it fits behind the saw, where it acts as an outfeed table extension.

FRED SOTCHER is a retired electrical engineer and an avid woodworker who lives in San Jose, California.

Stack and Saw Lumber on the Same Rack

BY CHRIS GOCHNOUR

Storing lumber effectively is a challenge in any shop, but it's especially challenging in a small shop. When I designed my current lumber rack, the efficient use of space was a priority. I wanted my lumber to be accessible and close to the chopsaw, where I cut it to rough length. Gradually, I developed the notion of a combination crosscutting table and lumber rack. While I was at it, I decided to make the chopsaw easily removable so that I could take it to installations.

The rack's framework consists of two hardwood posts and a series of cantilevered arms that hold the lumber and support the crosscutting table. The posts are lag-bolted to the stud wall. I chose bolts long enough to give me 3 in. of threads in the studs, and I mounted the posts 6 ft. apart to correspond with the wall studs.

The arms, also hardwood, are tenoned into the posts and secured with glue and draw-bored pegs. I chose to taper the arms so that I could have the strength of a large

CANTILEVERED ARMS AND A BUILT-IN CHOPSAW TABLE provide plenty of storage, easy access, and efficient crosscutting in a small space.

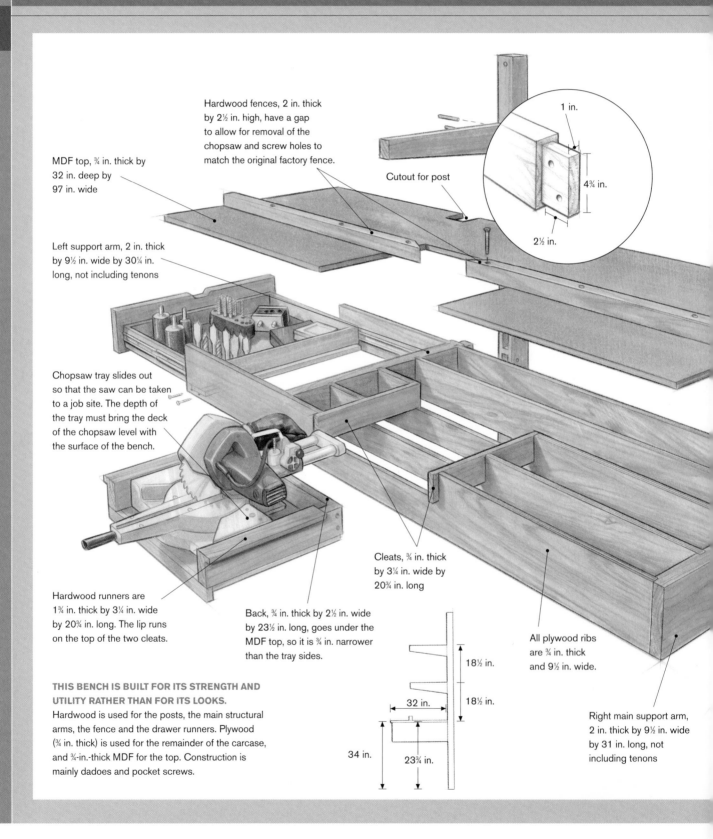

Hardwood fences, 2 in. thick by 2½ in. high, have a gap to allow for removal of the chopsaw and screw holes to match the original factory fence.

MDF top, ¾ in. thick by 32 in. deep by 97 in. wide

Cutout for post

1 in.

4¾ in.

2½ in.

Left support arm, 2 in. thick by 9½ in. wide by 30¼ in. long, not including tenons

Chopsaw tray slides out so that the saw can be taken to a job site. The depth of the tray must bring the deck of the chopsaw level with the surface of the bench.

Cleats, ¾ in. thick by 3¼ in. wide by 20¾ in. long

Hardwood runners are 1¾ in. thick by 3¼ in. wide by 20¾ in. long. The lip runs on the top of the two cleats.

Back, ¾ in. thick by 2½ in. wide by 23½ in. long, goes under the MDF top, so it is ¾ in. narrower than the tray sides.

All plywood ribs are ¾ in. thick and 9½ in. wide.

18½ in.

18½ in.

32 in.

34 in.

23¾ in.

Right main support arm, 2 in. thick by 9½ in. wide by 31 in. long, not including tenons

THIS BENCH IS BUILT FOR ITS STRENGTH AND UTILITY RATHER THAN FOR ITS LOOKS.
Hardwood is used for the posts, the main structural arms, the fence and the drawer runners. Plywood (¾ in. thick) is used for the remainder of the carcase, and ¾-in.-thick MDF for the top. Construction is mainly dadoes and pocket screws.

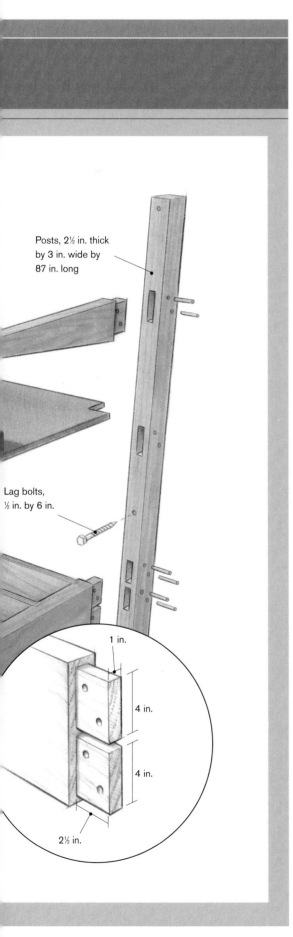

Posts, 2½ in. thick
by 3 in. wide by
87 in. long

Lag bolts,
½ in. by 6 in.

1 in.

4 in.

4 in.

2½ in.

tenon mounted into the posts but more room for lumber on the outside. For ease of assembly, I glued the arms into the posts before bolting the posts to the wall.

The arms that support the crosscutting table are almost twice the width of the others and are not tapered. I modified the joinery for these arms, stacking two tenons for each arm rather than making a very wide one. This improves the joint because less material is removed from the post, which minimizes the risk of splitting. It also avoids wood-movement problems that can occur with wide tenons.

The arms for the chopsaw table have a series of dadoes cut on the inside faces to accept plywood ribs that support the table-top. I made the top of the table out of medium-density fiberboard (MDF), because it is very flat and a good utility work surface. I also built a hardwood fence with stops for repetitive cutoff work.

The chopsaw is mounted on a small tray that slides into place and is secured with two screws. With this setup, I can remove the two bolts and take the saw with me.

In the shop, my fence replaces the factory fence. But when I take the saw on the road, I remount the factory fence.

My drill press is just a few feet away from the table, so I installed a drawer at one end to hold drill bits along with the drill-press accessories.

My rack is just inside the large door I use for bringing lumber into the shop. I simply back in my truck and unload lumber right onto the rack. And I let the work begin.

CHRIS GOCHNOUR is a furniture maker in Salt Lake City, Utah.

Convertible Clamping Workstation

BY GARY B. FOSTER

After working for months on my knees building a large bookcase, I decided I needed a low table in my shop for assembling large projects. Although my newly built shop is spacious at 1,040 sq. ft., I didn't want to take up room with a low table that would find only part-time use. It needed to do more. So I designed a workstation that also fulfilled a number of other shop needs, such as a place to store my clamps and to glue up furniture parts. The workstation is built in two sections and can be reconfigured to accommodate its various uses.

A Twist on the Torsion Box

The lower portion of the workstation is constructed as a tall torsion box. A plywood grid makes up its interior, consisting of five panels running widthwise and three longer panels running lengthwise. The panels, which stand on end, cross one another with crosslap joints, and they are sandwiched between two ¾-in.-thick plywood skins. Built into the lower torsion box is a web of PVC pipes that hold clamps up to 6 ft. long.

MOBILE WORKSTATION WITH CLAMP STORAGE. The lower portion of the workstation is a tall torsion box, consisting of a grid with five panels spanning the width and three panels spanning the length. The panels stand on end and cross one another with crosslap joints. The grid is sandwiched between two ¾-in.-thick plywood skins and is held together with glue and 2½-in. long gold drywall screws.

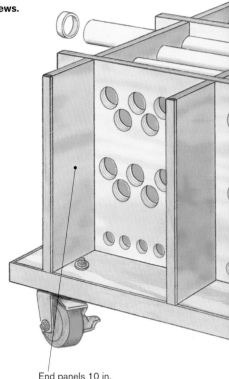

End panels 10 in. high by 35 in. long

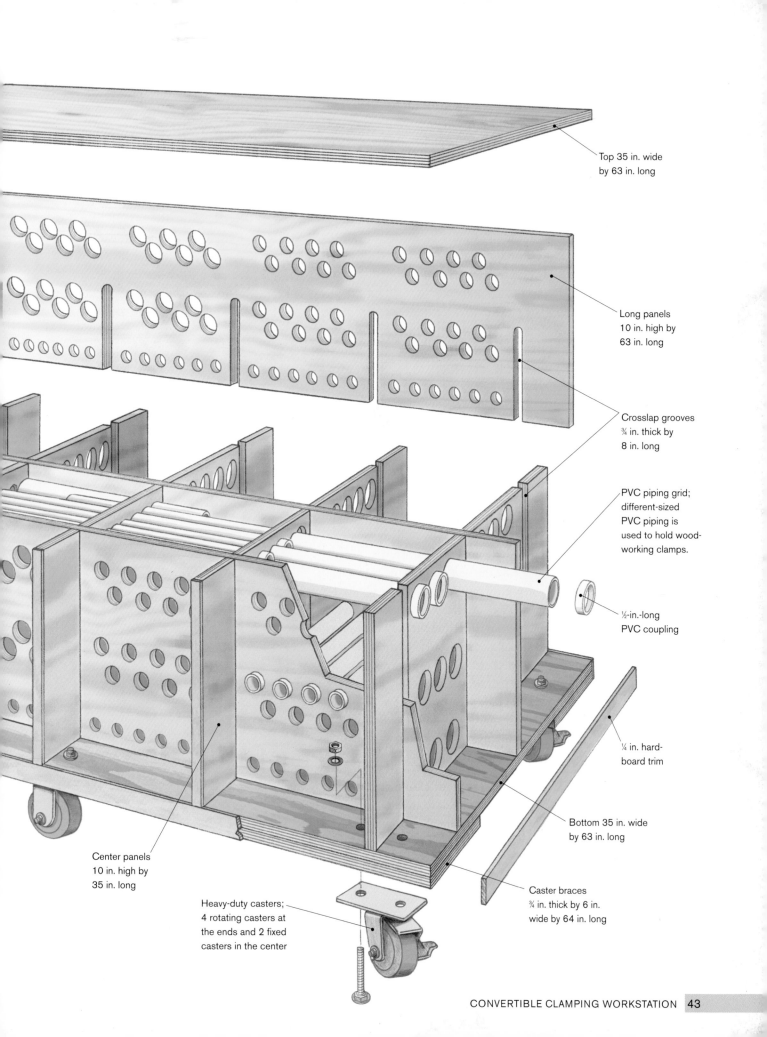

Top 35 in. wide by 63 in. long

Long panels 10 in. high by 63 in. long

Crosslap grooves ¾ in. thick by 8 in. long

PVC piping grid; different-sized PVC piping is used to hold woodworking clamps.

½-in.-long PVC coupling

¼ in. hardboard trim

Center panels 10 in. high by 35 in. long

Bottom 35 in. wide by 63 in. long

Heavy-duty casters; 4 rotating casters at the ends and 2 fixed casters in the center

Caster braces ¾ in. thick by 6 in. wide by 64 in. long

Build It from the Bottom Up Begin by cutting the crosslap joints in the plywood panels with a ¾-in. plywood router bit. This specialty bit, available from most home centers or catalog retailers, is slightly undersize to account for the actual thickness of plywood. Using this bit will make the crosslap joints fit tightly.

Next, plan and lay out the PVC piping. I chose to use several different-diameter pipes to hold the different clamps I own. The pipes extend through the torsion box's interior grid, and holes must be drilled in each plywood panel in the same location so that the pipes can feed through properly. I created a template to locate and drill pilot holes in each of the interior panels and then bored each hole with an appropriately sized hole saw.

After the plywood panels are prepared, begin assembling the torsion box. It must be constructed on a flat surface and upside down. Fit together the plywood grid and attach the bottom skin with glue and 2½-in.-long gold drywall screws.

While the box is upside down, attach six heavy-duty casters with carriage bolts. I applied an extra strip of plywood between the bottom panel and the casters to provide added strength for carrying the weight of the table as it's rolled around the shop. I used 6-in. casters rated at 700 lb., purchased from an industrial-supply store. The four corner casters spin and the two center casters are fixed, making the workstation easy to maneuver around the shop.

Plumb the table for clamp storage Flip over the torsion box to install the piping and the top skin. Install the lowest row of piping first and work your way up the table. To secure the pipes, purchase PVC couplings from any plumbing-supply store and cut the couplings into ½-in. rings on a bandsaw while holding them with locking pliers to keep them straight.

Plywood Panels

PVC pipes, with diameters based on the size of the clamps they will hold, feed through holes drilled in the plywood panels. Lay out the pipes so that those running through the width of the table don't interfere with those running lengthwise. Prepare a template to cut matching hole patterns on each plywood panel.

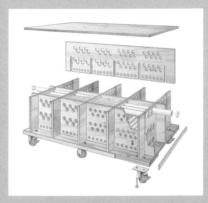

PREPARE TEMPLATES FOR MATCHING HOLES. The author makes templates with the center point drilled for transferring the hole pattern to each of the plywood panels.

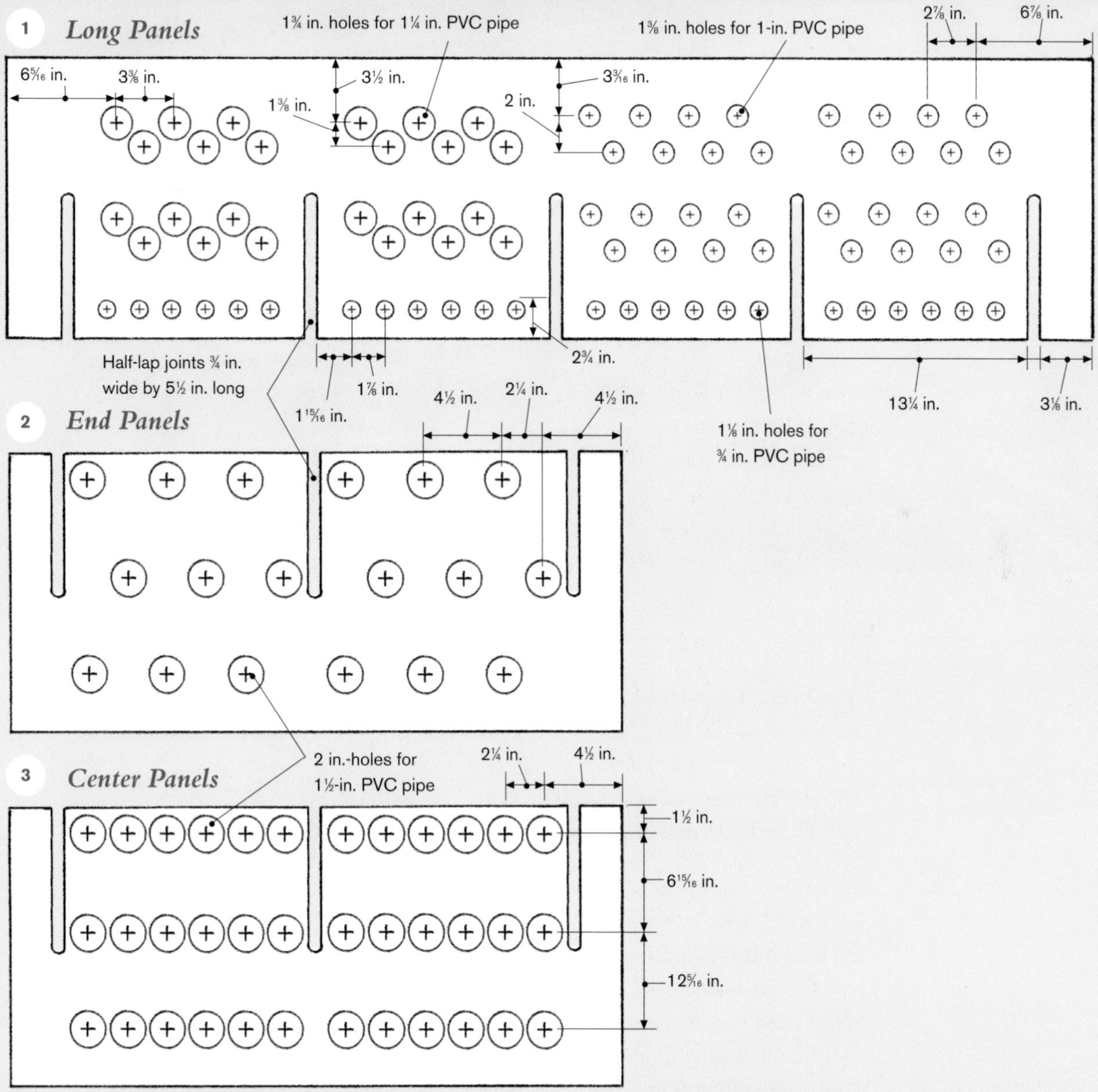
1 Long Panels
1¾ in. holes for 1¼ in. PVC pipe
1⅜ in. holes for 1-in. PVC pipe
2⅞ in.
6⅞ in.
6$\frac{5}{16}$ in.
3⅜ in.
3½ in.
1⅜ in.
2 in.
3$\frac{3}{16}$ in.
Half-lap joints ¾ in. wide by 5½ in. long
1⅞ in.
1$\frac{15}{16}$ in.
2¾ in.
13¼ in.
3⅛ in.
1⅛ in. holes for ¾ in. PVC pipe
2 End Panels
4½ in.
2¼ in.
4½ in.
3 Center Panels
2 in.-holes for 1½-in. PVC pipe
2¼ in.
4½ in.
1½ in.
6$\frac{15}{16}$ in.
12$\frac{9}{16}$ in.

MAKE CLAMP-HOLDER OUT OF PVC PIPE AND PVC COUPLINGS

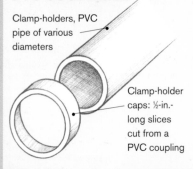

Clamp-holders, PVC pipe of various diameters

Clamp-holder caps: ½-in.-long slices cut from a PVC coupling

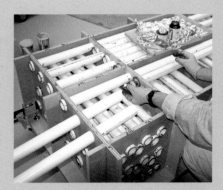

CONNECTING THE MAZE OF PIPING. Install the lowest row of piping first and work your way to the top.

SPACE-SAVING CLAMP STORAGE. PVC pipes, running through the length and width of the table, house clamps up to 6 ft. long.

The pipes spanning the width of the table are 1 in. longer than the width of the torsion box and project ½ in. at both ends. Glue a ring over one end of the PVC pipe and feed it through the plywood grid. The pipe should extend ½ in. from the other side of the table. Cap that end with a ½-in. ring.

The pipes spanning the length of the table are installed from both sides of the table but are accessible only from one end. These pipes should be cut roughly 10 in. shorter than the length of the torsion box.

Cap off one end of the pipe with a ½-in. ring and feed it through the table.

Clamp Table Makes Glue-Up Easy

The upper section of the table stacks on top of the lower section and is designed to support clamps when you assemble furniture parts. It also is constructed as a tall torsion box with panels that lock together with crosslap joints. However, this torsion box is not glued, so it can be reconfigured to hold clamps in different arrangements. Use a standard ¾-in. straight router bit when cutting the crosslap joints so that the plywood panels have wiggle room for assembly and disassembly. While most of the table is finished with oil-based polyurethane, these boards should be finished with a water-based polyurethane and waxed regularly to keep them from sticking.

To secure the upper section to the bottom, I installed four ⅜-in. wood dowels in each corner of the upper torsion box and drilled matching holes in the top surface of the lower table assembly.

Grooves hold clamps level On the top edge of the plywood panels, grooves are cut at regular intervals and sized to hold clamps. I've designed my table to hold Bessey K-body clamps and Jorgensen I-bar clamps (see "Sources"), so the grooves cut in the top edge of the plywood panels are sized for those. Grooves can be cut for clamps from any manufacturer. Size them

SIZING THE PLYWOOD GROOVES

Grooves for Jorgensen I-bar clamps: ½ in. thick by 1⅜ in. long

Melamine top: ¾ in. thick by 36 in. wide by 64 in. long

⅜ in.-dowels are inserted into holes to align and hold the melamine top on the grid below.

Lengthwise panels: ¾ in. thick by 10 in. wide by 63 in. long

13¼ in.

3⅛ in.

Grooves for I-bar clamps: ½ in. thick by 1⅜ in. long

Crosslap grooves ¾ in. thick by 5½ in. long

Two cross members have deep grooves on their bottom edge.

Shallow grooves for Bessey K-body clamps: ⅜ in. wide by 1⅛ in. deep

14 in.

2⅜ in.

Deep grooves for Bessey K-body clamps ⅜ in. wide by 2⅜ in. deep

Widthwise panels ¾ in. thick by 10 in. wide by 35 in. long

Dowels inserted into holes align and hold the grid to the base below.

ADD GRID FOR EFFICIENT CLAMPING. Similar to the lower section of the workstation, the upper section is a torsion box made of tall plywood panels joined with crosslap joints. However, they are not glued and are designed to be reconfigured. Grooves cut into the top edge of the plywood panels support clamps during glue-up. In one configuration, grooves spanning the width of the table are twice as deep as those spanning the length. This allows clamps to be arranged front to back and side to side without interference.

SETUP FOR LARGE PANELS

CROSSLAP JOINTS MAKE FOR EASY ASSEMBLY AND DISASSEMBLY OF PLYWOOD GRID. **Bar clamps rest in grooves cut into the top edge of the plywood grid. The clamps extend ⅛ in. above the plywood edge to provide clearance during glue-up.**

so that the width of the groove is equal to the width of the clamp, and the height of the groove is ⅛-in. shallower than the height of the clamp. As a result, the clamp will sit proud by ⅛ in. and keep a workpiece out of contact with the table during glue-up.

To accommodate two-directional clamping, grooves spanning the width of the table can be cut twice as deep as those along the length of the table. This way, the two clamps won't come in contact with each other when they cross. Two-directional clamping is necessary when gluing up a furniture part such as a frame-and-panel door, which requires clamping pressure on all four edges.

SETUP FOR PANEL DOORS

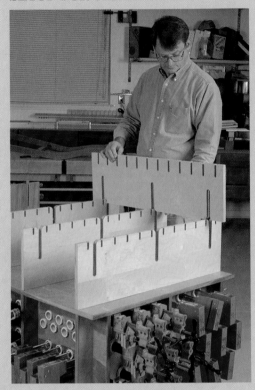

RECONFIGURING THE GRID FOR DIFFERENT CLAMPS AND FOR TWO DIRECTIONS. Deep grooves cut into the short plywood parts are sized to fit Bessey K-body clamps. The clamps situated front to back are set in deeper grooves than the clamps running left to right. This allows for cross clamping such objects as frame-and-panel doors.

Top Off the Table with a Sheet of Melamine

The upper section also can be used as a work surface by laying a sheet of ¾-in.-thick melamine on top of the plywood grid. With the top on, the table is level with my workbench and tablesaw, so it is useful as an infeed or outfeed support.

Again, install four wood dowels on the underside of the top sheet. Matching holes are drilled into the top edge of the upper torsion box and keep the work surface locked in position.

GARY B. FOSTER is a longtime woodworker and manages the tools department at the Lowe's in his hometown of Folsom, California.

Low Assembly Bench

BY BILL NYBERG

My father learned woodworking in Sweden, and when he came to this country, he got a job building reproduction Early American furniture. The shop had been in operation since the late 1700s, and like those who worked before him, my father was assigned a huge bench with many drawers. He stored his tools and ate his lunch at the bench, but much of his actual work took place nearby on a low table he called "the platform."

When I inherited his big bench, I also found myself doing most of my work at a low platform improvised from sawhorses and planks. I have bad shoulders and the occasional sore back, so using a full-height bench is difficult and unproductive. I needed a bench that suited the way I really work, so I built a low platform that incorporates some features of a traditional full-sized bench.

A Clamping Machine

My low platform bench is made for clamping (see the photos on p. 51). The edges overhang enough for clamps to get a good grip anywhere along the length of the bench. A 4-in.-wide space down the middle increases the clamping options.

VERSATILE PLATFORM puts your work at the right height.

50

This platform bench has four tail vises made from Pony® No. 53 double-pipe clamps (see "Sources"), which can be used by themselves or in combination with a row of dogs on the centerline between the screws, as the drawing on the following pages shows. Unlike most bench arrangements, with a single row of dogs along one edge, this one doesn't twist or buckle the piece. I can use each vise singly or with the others because the pipes are pinned into the benchtops at each end with ¼-in. by 2-in. roll pins. Without the pins, the pipes would slide through the bench when you tighten one end.

Rather than using traditional square bench dogs, I bored ¾-in. holes for a variety of manufactured dog fixtures or shopmade dowel dogs (see the drawing on pp. 52–53).

Building the Benchtops

The bench is made from eight straight, clear 8-ft. 2x4s that I had kept in the shop for a few months to dry. I jointed the edges and then ran each of the boards through the planer until the radiused corners were square.

Building the legs and base according to the dimensions on the drawing is straightforward. The only point to note is the dovetail connecting the beams to the legs. Because of the orientation of the beams and legs, the dovetail is only 1½ in. at its widest point, but it's 3½ in. from top to bottom. I tilted the tablesaw blade to cut the tails on the beam and cut the pins on the legs in the bandsaw. Almost any method would work to join the beam to the leg; my first version of the bench used a bolted slip joint.

The pipes run through the tops The tops are made in two sections and glued up with the pipes and vises in place. The upper sections are made of three boards and the lower section from two. I edge-glued them with alternating growth rings to eliminate cup-

Make Clamping Easy

TWO VISES THAT CAN BE ADJUSTED independently hold even irregular shapes securely.

THE OPEN SPACE AT THE CENTER OF THE BENCH allows clamping pressure to be applied anywhere.

ping. I cut ⅞-in. grooves lengthwise in the top face of the bottom section to accommodate the pipes.

The tops are held to each beam with a single lag screw, which allows seasonal movement. To lock the tops into the base, I cut dadoes on the lower faces of the bottom sections to fit over the beams.

LOW ASSEMBLY BENCH

A low bench made for clamping

This bench is 24 in. high, a convenient height for working on many projects. The benchtops are 42½ in. long, which gives more than 4 ft. between the jaws. At about 70 lbs., the bench is light enough to move around yet heavy enough for stability.

Bench dogs are hardwood dowels, ¾ in. in dia. and about 4½ in. long, planed flat on one side.

Cut off one side of handle. When the vise is open, gravity will keep the remaining portion of the handle below the benchtop.

10 in.

Pipe

Bench

Lag screw

A ¼-in. bullet catch keeps the dog in place.

Roll pins, ¼ in. by 2 in., keep pipe from turning.

Top assembly is dadoed ¼ in. deep to fit over beam.

Dowels align top during glue-up.

Roll p

Lag screws, ⅜ in. by 5 in. through beam

Leg braces are resawn 2x4s, about 1 1/16 in. by 3⅜ in.

Sources

(Pony Clamps)
www.adjustableclamps.com

Assembling the double-pipe clamps

The double-pipe clamps are sold with a tail stop and a screw head. I set aside the tail-stop ends and used only the screw heads. Threading on the vise at one end of the pipe will unscrew the vise at the other end. So I had a plumber cut the threads twice as long on one end of each of the four pipes. I threaded the first vise all the way onto the end with double-long threads so that it was twice as far on the pipe as it needed to go. By the time the second vise was in place, the first one had unscrewed itself to the correct location.

Keep ends flush when gluing

Before the pipes are installed in the grooves, I cut all the bench pieces to length. Once the tops are glued up, the pipes and vises are in the way, so it's hard to trim up ends that aren't flush. For flush ends, I aligned the pieces with dowel pins between top and bottom. I applied the glue and clamped the top and bottom sections together with the dowels

in place. After the glue was dry, I drilled for the roll pins from the bottom so they wouldn't show.

BILL NYBERG is director of ophthalmic photography at the University of Pennsylvania in Philadelphia. He works wood in his spare time.

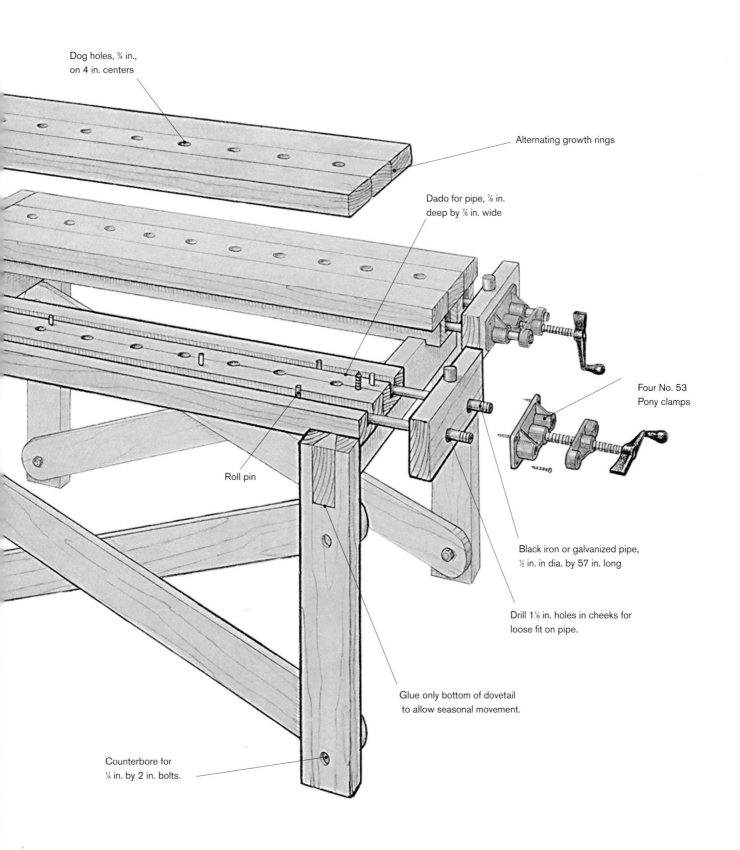

Dog holes, ¾ in.,
on 4 in. centers

Alternating growth rings

Dado for pipe, ⅞ in.
deep by ⅞ in. wide

Four No. 53
Pony clamps

Roll pin

Black iron or galvanized pipe,
½ in. in dia. by 57 in. long

Drill 1⅛ in. holes in cheeks for
loose fit on pipe.

Glue only bottom of dovetail
to allow seasonal movement.

Counterbore for
¼ in. by 2 in. bolts.

Vacuum Hold-Down Table

BY MIKE M. McCALLUM

When I'm constructing a set of custom cabinets, I frequently need an extra pair of hands, especially when I'm sanding drawer fronts or drilling odd-shaped pieces. Occasionally, I also need a table-mounted router. More often than not, I require that router table or that pair of hands at a job site. After putting up with cobbled scraps, makeshift clamps and excessive router dust one too many times, I came up with a design for a router table that's also a vacuum hold-down. Using scrap materials, I built the table so that I could easily disassemble it for storage or transport.

I call my knockdown platform a super router/hold-down table for a couple of reasons. First, it's stout, turning my router into a light-capacity shaper. Second, it enables my shop vacuum to serve dual functions by providing suction for the hold-down surface or collecting dust from the router table. And while I don't use the hold-down to freehand-rout large workpieces, I do rely on its substantial holding power for most of my sanding and finishing work (see the photo on p. 56).

Design and Construction

The dimensions of the hold-down table are not critical, but be sure to adjust for the size of your work area, vacuum hose, and router. I made my table out of ⅝-in. high-density particleboard and covered exposed surfaces with scraps of plastic laminate. The top is removable, so I can use the vacuum table on my benchtop. I stiffened the table's top and bottom by gluing on a particleboard framework, as shown in the drawing on the facing page. The top and bottom frames hold the sides and center divider in place without fasteners, allowing easy knockdown of the unit. After assembling the top and bottom oversized, I trimmed the parts square. I laminated all the pieces, and then I bored two holes in the edge of the table, so I can connect my shop vacuum to either the router-table or hold-down side (see the photo on p. 56). To power the table, I ran a heavy-duty extension cord to a 4x4 electrical box and mounted the box's stud bracket to the inside of the platform. The box houses switched receptacles for both the router (or sander) and shop vacuum. I also added a plywood shelf (see the photo on p. 57) to the table to hold tools, bits, guide bushings, and adapters. I ordered most of these accessories through MLCS Ltd. (see "Sources" on p. 56).

54

KNOCKDOWN SANDING AND ROUTING PLATFORM

All ⅝-in. high-density particleboard, unless noted

Laminate top

Hold-down holes,
¹⁄₆₄-in. dia., have chamfered
edges. Pattern matches
tree-shaped chamber.

Router insert

Rout tree-shaped
chamber at stepped depths
(see chamber detail).

Particleboard
framework

Vacuum
hook-up holes

Plywood shelf

Caulk Lexan window
into ¼-in.-deep
routed flange.

Sides, 13 in. high by
14 in. wide

Heavy-duty extension
cord connects to
4 in. by 4 in. electrical
box for switched
receptacles.

Pine rail, 1 in. by 5 in.

Top and bottom frames
are 1½ in. by 17 in. by
30 in. Overall height of
tables is 16 in.

Pine shelf cleats

Apply plastic laminate
to exposed surfaces.

Detail: Air Channels

Air channels, ½ in. wide, are routed in shallower steps the farther
they are from the vacuum outlet, to ensure even vacuum pressure.

VACUUM SIDE HAS PLENTY OF CLAMPING POWER. The vacuum surface (left) clamps a drawer front as the author sands its face. An open hole on the edge of the table (right) shows where he connects his shop vacuum when he's routing.

Sources

Lexan
800-752-7842
www.gelexan.com

MLCS
P.O. Box 4053
Rydal, PA 19046
800-533-9298
www.mlcswoodwork-
ing.com

Oak Park Enterprises
Box 280
Elie, Manitoba
ROH OHO
Canada
800-665-0252

The Router-Table Side

I made a clear window for the router table from Lexan® (see "Sources"), which I recycled from a computer-store display. The window is a good safety feature because it lets in enough light to see the collet when I'm adjusting the bit height or using the router table. The router insert is a standard one—it fits whatever bit I'm using. Oak Park Enterprises, Ltd. (see "Sources") carries complete bearing and insert kits for various router models. To prevent vibration and flush the router-table surface, I oiled the insert's bearing surface and then caulked the face of the insert with silicone before I placed it into the flange that I had routed into the tabletop. I clamped the assembly flat on my tablesaw. In use, I estimate that my 5-gal. collector sucks up about 50 percent of the dust from the router. I'm sure that with a few provisions, such as adding intake holes, I could improve the dust-collection capability considerably.

The Hold-Down Side

On a piece of tracing paper, I drew an evenly spaced tree-shaped hole pattern that was suitable for my hold-down needs. After I transferred the tree pattern onto the particleboard top, I freehand routed the air channels for the vacuum chamber. To ensure an even vacuum across the hold-down surface, I routed the channels at ascending depths (see the air-channel detail in the drawing). I based the stepped depths on vacuum-drop ratios for the chamber volume. If you're using plywood for the table, paint or seal the routed pattern to prevent air leaks before you glue on the laminate. To make the hole pattern in the laminate, I first placed a clear piece of plastic over the routed chamber and poked out

TO WIRE HIS TABLE, the author fed a 4-in. work box for a pair of switched receptacles: one for the vacuum, one for a router or sander. A shelf at the back of the table holds tools and accessories. He drew outlines of the items and routed recesses to hold each shape, which reminds him when something's missing.

a hole pattern to follow the air-channel shape. Then I used a crayon to rub the hole locations onto the laminate. When boring through the laminate, use a tiny bit (I used a ⅟₆₄-in. twist drill). The small orifices, through the Venturi principle, increase the vacuum. Finally, lightly countersink the holes.

Using the Vacuum Hold-Down

As long as my workpiece has a flat surface to put down on the hold-down table, I've found that there's plenty of suction—enough to grip a piece of low-grade ply-wood. To increase the holding pressure, you could also block off holes that are not covered by the workpiece. On rough surfaces, I take a ⅛-in.-thick piece of closed-cell plastic (shipper's foam) to make a gasket. With a utility knife, I cut out an appropriate shape that still allows the vacuum to suck the

workpiece down. I use a couple of pieces of masking tape to hold the gasket to the table. If you need to hold down a sphere, an odd shape, or a piece with a very uneven surface, you can make a holder as follows: Sculpt out a Styrofoam® gasket for the shape you want to secure. In a well-ventilated area or outdoors, heat up a piece of nichrome or small stainless-steel wire with a propane torch, so you can make a series of holes through the gasket. Tape the Styrofoam to the hold-down table, and you've got a fairly quick clamp to hold just about any shape that you have to sand or drill holes in. So far, I've been delighted with the possibilities of the hold-down table. In fact, I'm work-ing on a sliding saw table that uses a similar vacuum hold-down system.

MIKE McCALLUM is an artist who does custom architectural woodworking in Portland, Oregon.

Rolling Chopsaw Stand Saves Space

BY CHARLES JACOBY

My shop is pretty crowded, so when I acquire a new tool, I have to create efficient ways to store and use the tool. Such was the case after I bought a new sliding compound-miter saw. The saw needed a permanent, but mobile, home where I could do accurate cutoff and miter work. I first tried using the saw on planks and horses. This worked fine for single cuts, but I really needed a fence with a stop for cutting multiples. And the extensions that came with the saw limited its cutting to short pieces. Also, I still had to break things down to put the saw away.

About this time, my wife, Rosemary, gave me a benchtop oscillating-spindle sander. Again I wondered where I would store the tool. Building a stand to house both tools was the answer—make that a movable stand with folding extension wings. I designed the stand with crosscutting and mitering in mind but with a place to store the sander. I also left room for a top drawer to hold my shaper cutters and accessories. When I'm not using the saw, I drop the wings and roll the stand into a corner (see the photo on the facing page). And even with the wings folded down, I can still do short chopsaw work by clamping a stop block to the saw's auxiliary fence.

Cabinet Construction

For the stand's carcase, I made a ¾-in. birch-plywood box. To make storing the sander easy, I left the stand's lower compartment open (back and front). I dadoed the box's top, middle and bottom ¼ in. into the sides. Then, using #10 biscuits and glue, I plate-joined maple face frames to the front and back of the carcase to make the box rigid. Because my miter saw has its own base with four feet, I recessed the top of the cabinet so that the saw's work surface would be at the same height as the wings (see the drawing on p. 60). I also fastened four 2½-in.-dia. casters (two of them locking) to hardwood plates that I glued to the bottom of the cabinet. The added height of the casters puts the top of the stand at a comfortable working level. To protect the top edges of the plywood sides, I mounted strips of ¾ x ¾ aluminum angle.

Collapsible Wings

What makes the stand accurate and maneuverable are the folding pair of wings attached to the side of the cabinet. Each wing basically consists of a table, a support, and a fence. The tables are ¾-in. plywood, and the supports are made from ½-in.-thick Baltic-birch plywood for strength. To stiffen the

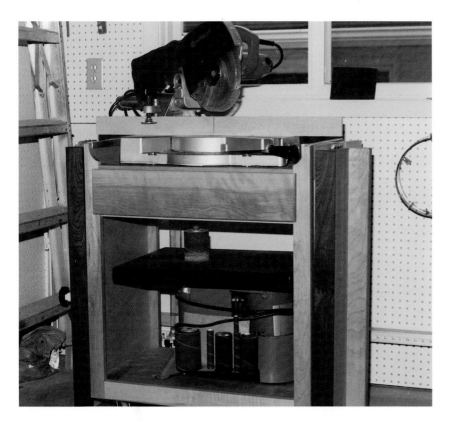

wing tables, I made front rails using walnut I had on hand. The wave-like curves of the supports aren't necessary, but I wanted to use my new spindle-sander. To strengthen the top of the supports, I glued and screwed on a maple block to the back side of each. Finally, I made the fence for each wing from two pieces of ¾-in. plywood, staggered and glued together to form a rabbet (see the drawing detail, p. 61). I glued and biscuited the fences' rabbets to the wing tables, and then I capped the top of the fences with mahogany. I chamfered the caps' edges, so there would be enough clearance for the runner block of an adjustable stop.

A Flip Stop for the Fence

By securing a flip stop to the left fence, I'm able to measure precise lengths. The stop I use is made by Biesemeyer Manufacturing Corp. (see "Sources"). I purposely made my fence higher than what the flip stop

requires to permit a full 2x4 to go under the stop. Because of the extra height, I had to make a metal stop extension to get it low enough for thin boards.

Aligning the Wings and Mounting the Saw

The collapsible wings are strong; I can crosscut 14-ft.-long 2x8s in half on a fully extended stand. To achieve this kind of load, I had to first add blocks and stiffeners to reinforce the cabinet where the wing-table and wing-support hinges attach. I secured 1¾-in.-thick support blocks to the top of the cabinet sides. Then I fastened ¾-in.-thick strips of maple to the plywood sides. For the hinges, I fastened two Corbin ball-bearing (large door) hinges to the wing tables and then mounted a pair of 2-in. by 24-in. piano hinges to the wing supports.

Before I screwed the hinges to the cabinet, I lined up the tables and fences as follows: First, I propped each wing assembly in

ANATOMY OF A MOBILE CHOPSAW STAND

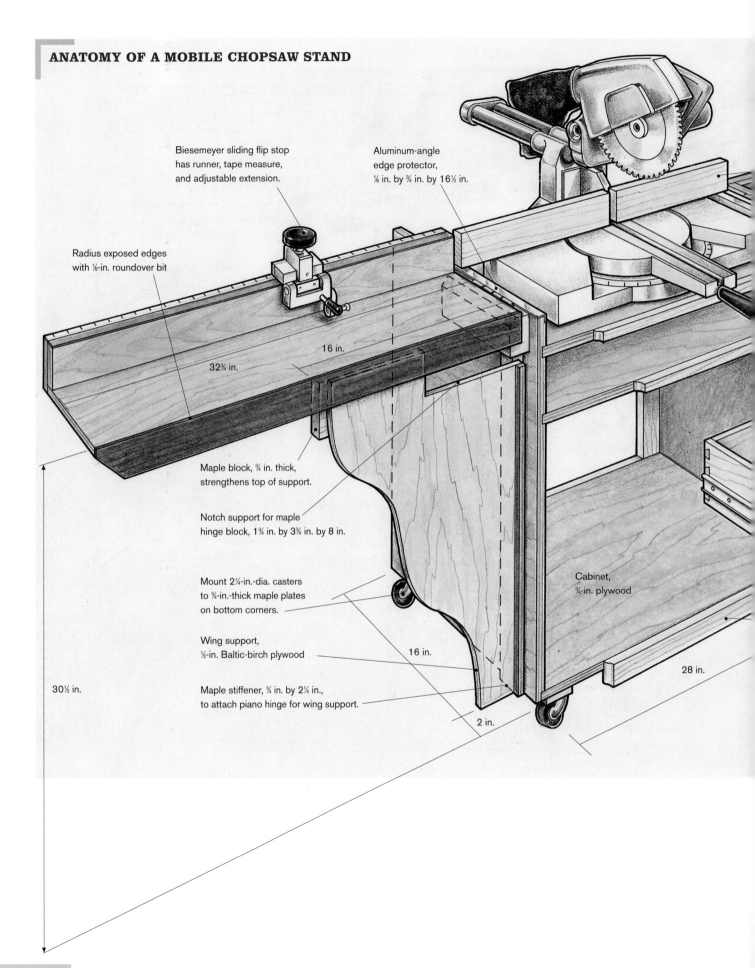

Biesemeyer sliding flip stop has runner, tape measure, and adjustable extension.

Aluminum-angle edge protector, ⅛ in. by ¾ in. by 16½ in.

Radius exposed edges with ⅛-in. roundover bit

16 in.

32¾ in.

Maple block, ¾ in. thick, strengthens top of support.

Notch support for maple hinge block, 1¾ in. by 3¾ in. by 8 in.

Mount 2¼-in.-dia. casters to ¾-in.-thick maple plates on bottom corners.

Wing support, ½-in. Baltic-birch plywood

Maple stiffener, ¾ in. by 2¼ in., to attach piano hinge for wing support.

Cabinet, ¾-in. plywood

16 in.

30½ in.

2 in.

28 in.

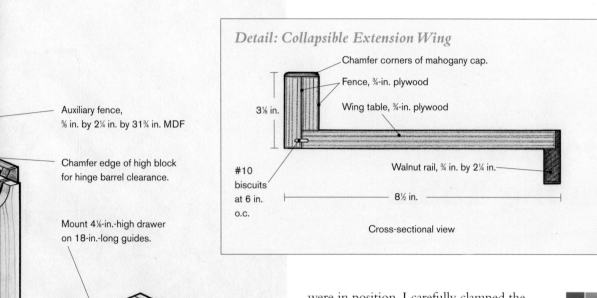

Detail: Collapsible Extension Wing

Chamfer corners of mahogany cap.

Fence, ¾-in. plywood

Wing table, ¾-in. plywood

3⅛ in.

#10 biscuits at 6 in. o.c.

Walnut rail, ¾ in. by 2¼ in.

8½ in.

Cross-sectional view

Auxiliary fence, ⅝ in. by 2¼ in. by 31¾ in. MDF

Chamfer edge of high block for hinge barrel clearance.

Mount 4⅛-in.-high drawer on 18-in.-long guides.

Maple face-frame, ¾ in. by 2 in., plate-joined to front and back of cabinet.

Total length of stand with both wings extended is 98 in. Align the face of the wing fences ⅛ in. back from face of auxiliary fence. Mount saw to stand with ⁵⁄₁₆-in. machine bolts and fender washers.

place with buckets and blocks. Next, I set my saw down at the rear of the cabinet top and laid a 6-ft.-long straightedge across the front of the fences. After I had shimmed each wing so its fence was properly aligned (an extra pair of hands is a big help), I flipped the straightedge 90° to set the height of the wing tables. Once the wings were in position, I carefully clamped the hinges in place, so I could make pilot holes. Finally, I screwed the table hinges to the support blocks and the piano hinges to the stiffener strips.

I offset the saw's auxiliary fence about ⅛ in. ahead of the wing fences so that they won't influence the alignment of long boards held snugly to the saw's fence. I fastened the saw to the cabinet top using ⁵⁄₁₆-in. machine bolts with large fender washers under the plywood. With the wings extended, I originally figured I'd have to clamp the supports to the front rails. But the wing tables are heavy and rest on the supports unaided.

Finishing Touches

To complete the stand, I made a simple drawer for the upper cabinet opening. Before installing the drawer on a pair of 18-in.-long slides, I notched the top of the drawer back to clear the ends of the saw-mounting bolts. Finally, I sealed the drawer, cabinet and wings with clear Watco® oil. Once my mobile stand was finished, I put the saw right to work, cutting everything from baseboard to pull out dish racks for the kitchen.

CHARLES JACOBY is a retired men's clothing store owner who enjoys making furniture for his family in Helena, Montana.

Sources

Biesemeyer Manufacturing Corp.
216 S. Alma School Road, Suite #3, Mesa, Arizona, 85210; 800-782-1831 www.biesemeyer.com

A Downdraft Sanding Table

BY PETER BROWN

THIS SHOPMADE UNIT CONQUERS **dust without breaking the bank.**

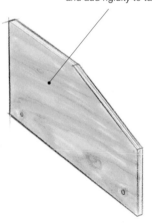

Side panels, ½ in. thick by 9 in. wide by 16½ in. long, limit airflow to top of table and add rigidity to table frame.

My shop was originally a 20-ft. by 40-ft. hog barn. In the early years, before it could really be called a shop, I conveniently ignored the dust created from sanding. However, after I added a floor and finished the interior, I became more conscious of the dust and began to take large sanding projects out to another barn, where I could let the dust fly. The solution was clear: I had to find some way to collect sanding dust.

When I first noticed downdraft sanding tables that were for sale, I was intrigued. They were just what I needed, but I could

SHOPMADE DOWNDRAFT TABLE

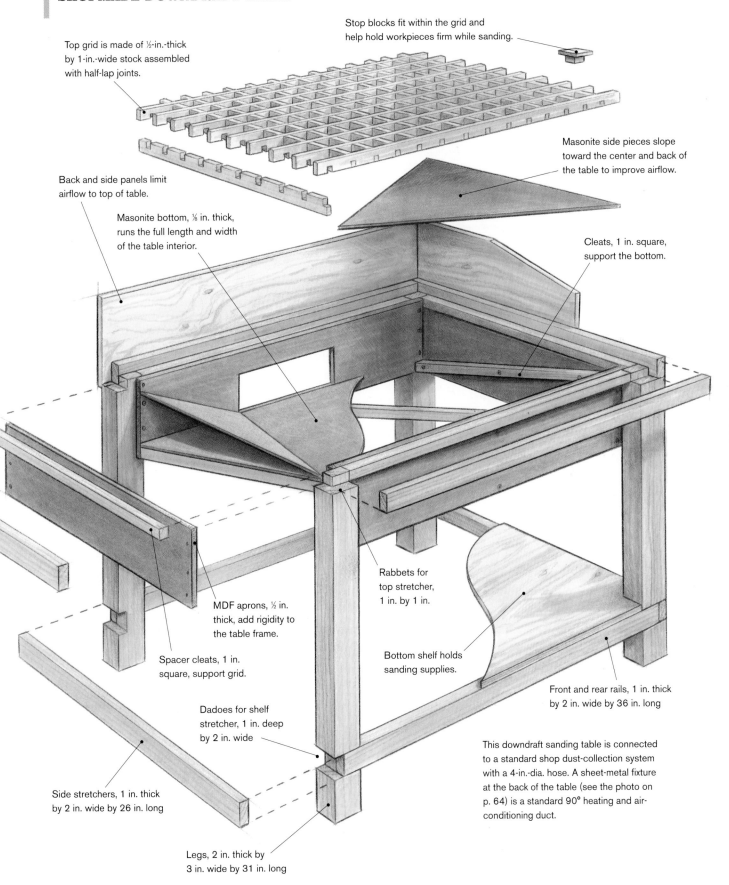

Top grid is made of ½-in.-thick by 1-in.-wide stock assembled with half-lap joints.

Stop blocks fit within the grid and help hold workpieces firm while sanding.

Back and side panels limit airflow to top of table.

Masonite side pieces slope toward the center and back of the table to improve airflow.

Masonite bottom, ⅛ in. thick, runs the full length and width of the table interior.

Cleats, 1 in. square, support the bottom.

MDF aprons, ½ in. thick, add rigidity to the table frame.

Rabbets for top stretcher, 1 in. by 1 in.

Spacer cleats, 1 in. square, support grid.

Dadoes for shelf stretcher, 1 in. deep by 2 in. wide.

Bottom shelf holds sanding supplies.

Front and rear rails, 1 in. thick by 2 in. wide by 36 in. long

Side stretchers, 1 in. thick by 2 in. wide by 26 in. long

This downdraft sanding table is connected to a standard shop dust-collection system with a 4-in.-dia. hose. A sheet-metal fixture at the back of the table (see the photo on p. 64) is a standard 90° heating and air-conditioning duct.

Legs, 2 in. thick by 3 in. wide by 31 in. long

AN INEXPENSIVE CONNECTION. Brown used a standard sheet-metal air-conditioning duct to tie the sanding table to his shop duct system.

calculated the area of the tabletop (864 sq. in.) and subtracted the area taken up by the grid material (330 sq. in.), leaving an open area of 534 sq. in. This is equivalent to a 26-in.-dia. duct, and I began to get a feeling that I might have a problem. With even a minimum 3,000-fpm velocity at the table, I would need a flow rate of more than 10,000 cfm. All of a sudden my central dust-collection system looked seriously inadequate.

Undaunted, I resolved to give it a try regardless of what the calculations told me. I decided to build the framework of the table and then make cardboard mock-ups of the interior to determine the best flow characteristics. I built the sanding table entirely from scraps, and the size of the scraps dictated the size of the components. After making the frame, I made the first mock-up of the table interior. The mock-up had a flat bottom with straight sides and an 8-in.-dia. duct at the bottom of the table. Regardless of what adjustments I made, the airflow wasn't evenly distributed across the table: It was fair near the outlet but poor elsewhere. For the second mock-up, I changed the outlet duct from the round to a standard 4-in. by 12-in. heating duct made of sheet metal, and I moved the outlet to the back of the table. I sloped the interior bottom from front to back and added the side pieces that slope toward the center and the back of the table.

The second mock-up made a significant improvement in the airflow, giving me good dust collection. I replaced the cardboard mock-up with ⅛-in.-thick Masonite. The addition of the ½-in.-thick MDF back and side apron pieces at the top of the table adds rigidity to the frame and keeps stray dust within the collection area.

PETER BROWN works as an engineer developing repairs for jet engines.

not afford any of them. It was then that I decided to make my own downdraft table utilizing the central dust-collection system in my shop. I use a shopmade system built with the motor and impeller from a portable Dust Boy—rated to move 1,100 cu. ft. of air per minute (cfm) at a velocity of 5,400 ft. per minute (fpm)—adapted to an Oneida Air Systems™ cyclone. I was confident that by locating my 2-hp Dust Boy close to the downdraft table, my system would do the job.

I based the size of the sanding tabletop —24 in. deep by 36 in. wide—on the average dimension of my workpieces. I then

Power-Tool Workbench

BY LARS MIKKELSEN

Space is at a premium in my small shop, so the more functions any one thing can serve the better. I had two things that needed improvement—my hand power tools were cramped in a small cabinet, their cords always entwined, and my bench needed a good base. So I decided to kill two birds with one stone and build a base cabinet for the bench with cubbies for my tools.

These cubbies have worked out very well for me. Each tool has its place, where I also keep the miscellaneous wrenches and screwdrivers needed for that particular tool. The small size of the cubbies makes the tools much easier to find than if they were stored on long shelves. The cords never get tangled, and it's so easy to get and put away a tool that I avoid the usual clutter on the benchtop. The power strip that I attached to the bench makes it possible for a tool to be in its cubby while still plugged in ready to go.

BENCH SLAVE HOLDS LONG STOCK. The author made a bench slave with a brace at the top that locks into the 1-in. dowel bench dogs he uses. Round dogs are easier to make and install than traditional square dogs.

Detail: Bench Slave

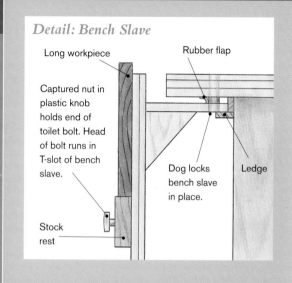

Long workpiece

Rubber flap

Captured nut in plastic knob holds end of toilet bolt. Head of bolt runs in T-slot of bench slave.

Dog locks bench slave in place.

Ledge

Stock rest

Building a Power-Tool Workbench

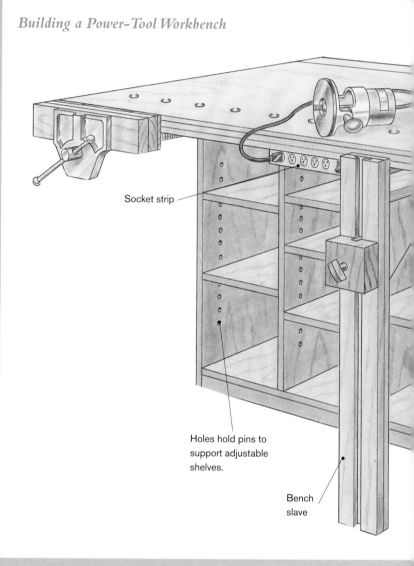

Socket strip

Holes hold pins to support adjustable shelves.

Bench slave

Quick-Access Tool Cubbies

I made the base cabinet from ¾-in. birch plywood edged with ¼-in. strips of solid birch and biscuited together, as shown in the drawing. The biscuits could be replaced with tongue-and-groove joints or dadoes and rabbets, but biscuits are the simplest. I measured my biggest tool to determine the maximum width and depth of the sections.

The desired final height of the benchtop sets the base height, and the shelves are adjustable. The dimensions can all be adapted to your own situation, but it is helpful to keep the combined width of the benchtop (mine is 29 in.) and depth of the base cabinet (mine is 18 in.) below the standard 48-in. width of a sheet of plywood, so you can use the cutoffs from ripping the top to

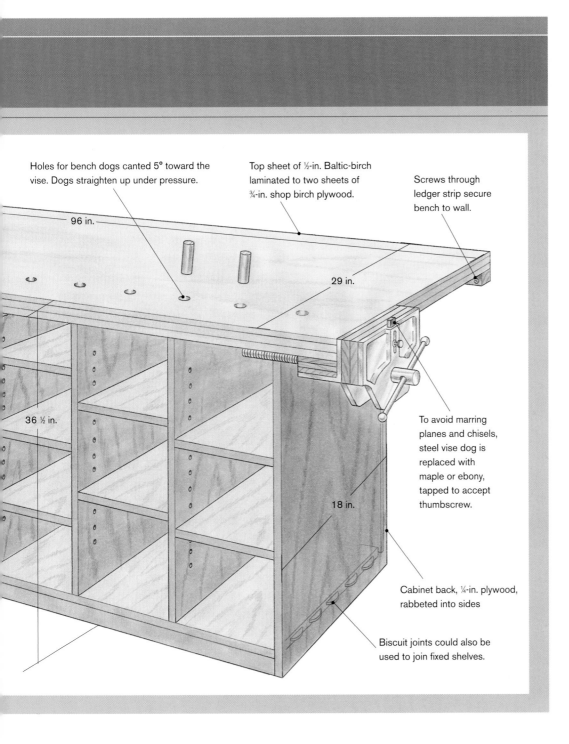

Holes for bench dogs canted 5° toward the vise. Dogs straighten up under pressure.

Top sheet of ½-in. Baltic-birch laminated to two sheets of ¾-in. shop birch plywood.

Screws through ledger strip secure bench to wall.

96 in.

29 in.

36 ½ in.

18 in.

To avoid marring planes and chisels, steel vise dog is replaced with maple or ebony, tapped to accept thumbscrew.

Cabinet back, ¼-in. plywood, rabbeted into sides

Biscuit joints could also be used to join fixed shelves.

make parts for the base. And while I used all the space for cubbies, one of the sections could easily be set up to hold simple sliding shelves for bit storage. The shelves could slide in dadoes cut across the width of facing vertical dividers before assembly.

I used ¼-in. plywood for the back of the base and anchored my bench to the wall with 3-in. screws driven through a ledger strip on the underside of the top. For a freestanding bench, I would recommend, at minimum, a ¾-in. back and a hefty face frame to add stiffness against racking. For maximum strength in a freestanding bench, cubbies could be made to fit beneath a traditional mortise–and–tenon trestle base.

A Plywood Work Surface

The top of my bench is made from two layers of ¾-in. shop-birch plywood and one layer of ½-in. Baltic-birch plywood. Unlike shop-birch plywood, which has a core of thick softwood veneers between thin outer layers of birch, Baltic birch is all birch with a core of thin, high-quality veneers, free of voids. (Baltic birch sheets are often sized metrically and will run approximately twice the cost of shop birch.★) This sandwich of shop birch and Baltic birch makes the benchtop amply stiff, and the Baltic birch has a surface hard enough and thick enough to withstand some abuse. I laminated the three sheets of plywood with Liquid Nails construction adhesive. I did not have any way of clamping something this big, so I used lots of screws coming up from the bottom. I removed the screws once the adhesive had set, so I wouldn't run into them later when drilling for the bench dogs or other fixtures.

A New Twist on Old Dogs

I mounted two Record® #52½ ED vises to the top, one as an end vise, the other as a front vise. Both have wooden jaw faces. I tapped the metal jaws, so I could change the wooden faces easily without removing the vises from the bench. The front vise has oversized jaws to get a better grip on large pieces. To make bench dogs, I cut up a 1-in.-dia. dowel. I drilled a series of 1-in. holes for the dogs in line with the end vise dog. The holes angle toward the vise at 5 degrees so the bench dogs straighten up under pressure. To keep the dogs from sliding down when in use, I tacked small strips of rubber to the underside of the bench, partially overlapping the dog holes. But I was afraid vigorous pounding on the bench might make the dogs fall out, so I screwed and glued a ledge to the base that supports the inside half of the dogs. I can easily reach under the bench to push the dogs up, and when not in use, they remain firm against the ledge.

Long Stock Support

For the times when I have a long piece of stock clamped in the front vise, I made a bench slave to support the free end (see the photo on p. 65). The outer face of the slave leg is in the same plane as the inner jaw of the shoulder vise. I use the bench dogs and the ledge beneath them as a way of locking the slave to the table. Instead of making it freestanding, with feet that might get in my way, I built a kind of peg leg with a brace near the top that slides under the benchtop and rests on the ledge beneath the bench dogs. I drilled a slightly oversized hole through the brace, so it can easily be locked in place under any of the bench dogs.

The stock rest, a block of solid wood, is attached to the leg with a toilet bolt that slides in a T-slot (as shown in the drawing detail on p. 66) and can be locked at any height on the slave. To make the leg, I cut a shallow groove in a piece of ¾-in. solid wood and glued it, grooved side in, to a piece of ½-in. plywood; then I cut a narrower groove in the outside face, forming a T-slot for the head of the toilet bolt. A spline glued into the back of the stock rest rides in the stem of the slot.

My bench was relatively inexpensive to build and serves my purpose well. I like the big top, and the vises can hold everything I work on, from big doors to the occasional miniature. Doors on a base like this might look good, but the ease of access would be lost, and in a shop, efficiency comes before aesthetics.

★ *Please note that price estimates are from 1993.*

LARS MIKKELSEN is a professional woodworker in Santa Margarita, California.

New-Fangled Workbench

BY JOHN WHITE

For five years I worked as a cabinet-maker in a shop that used only hand tools for the simple reason that electricity wasn't available that far back in the woods. One lesson that I came away with was the importance of a good work-bench—and lots of windows. I now work in a shop that is, if anything, overelectrified, but a functional workbench is still impor-tant. Just because you're driving a car instead of a buggy doesn't mean you don't need a good road to get where you're going.

On a perfect bench, the various vises and stops would hold any size workpiece in the most convenient position for the job at hand. Traditional workbenches are adequate for clamping smaller pieces, a table leg or frame rail, for instance, but most benches can't handle wide boards for edge- and face-planing or frame-and-panel assemblies.

Recently, I moved my shop and needed to build a new bench. I began by research-ing traditional American and European designs. I found that although our prede-cessors had many clever solutions to the problems of holding down a piece of wood, no one bench solved all or even most of the problems I had encountered in 25 years of woodworking. Frustrated, I finally decided to design a bench from the ground up.

At first I had no success. A design would address one problem but not another, or it would be far too complex. I was about to give up and build a traditional German bench when I came up with a design that incorporates pipe clamps into the bench's top, the front apron, and even the legs.

WITH SIX PIPE CLAMPS, SOME DRESSED FRAMING LUMBER, and a handful of hardware, you can make an inexpensive bench that's as versatile as a Swiss Army Knife.

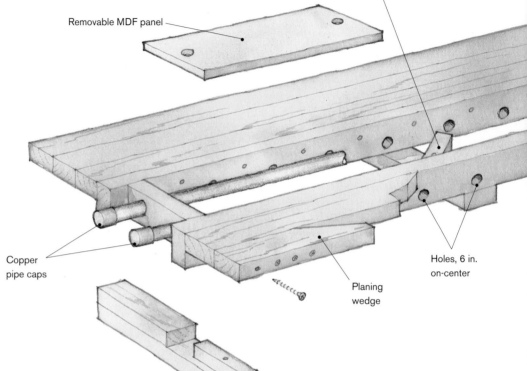

Pipe support blocks, fastened with single screws, turn to allow clamps to slide past.

Removable MDF panel

Copper
pipe caps

Planing
wedge

Holes, 6 in.
on-center

Overall dimensions
Height: 35½ in.
Width: 28 in.
Length: 96 in.
All wood: Douglas fir,
unless noted

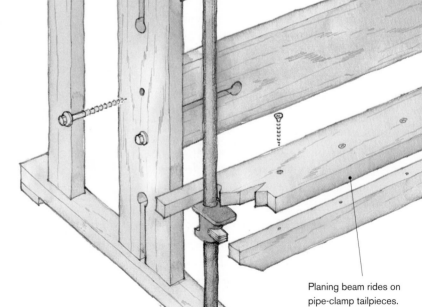

Planing beam rides on
pipe-clamp tailpieces.

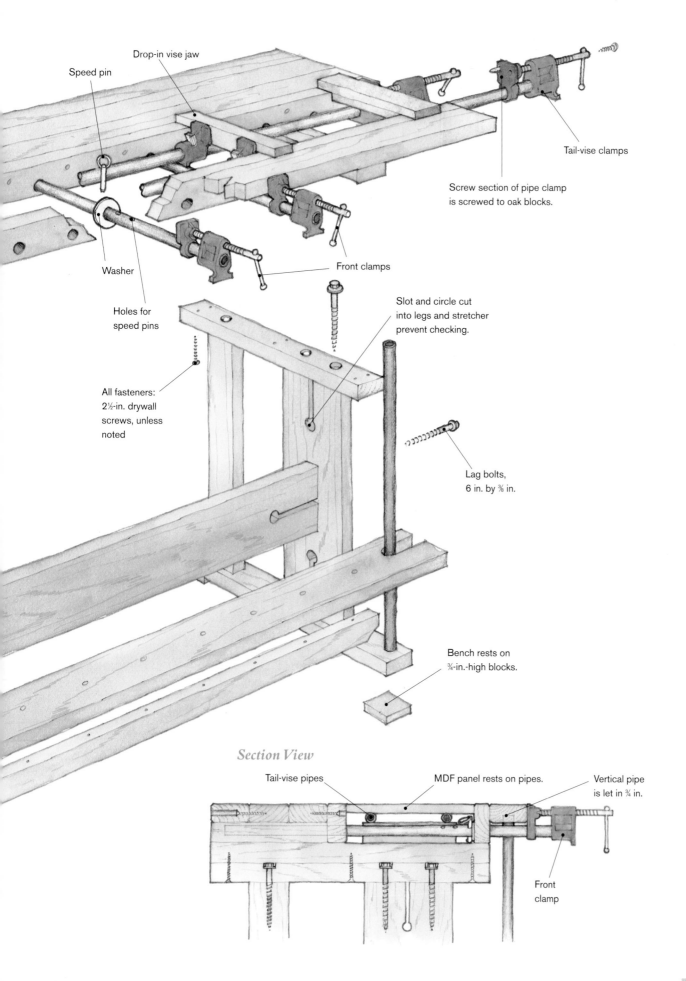

Speed pin

Drop-in vise jaw

Tail-vise clamps

Screw section of pipe clamp
is screwed to oak blocks.

Washer

Front clamps

Holes for
speed pins

Slot and circle cut
into legs and stretcher
prevent checking.

All fasteners:
2½-in. drywall
screws, unless
noted

Lag bolts,
6 in. by ⅜ in.

Bench rests on
¾-in.-high blocks.

Section View

Tail-vise pipes

MDF panel rests on pipes.

Vertical pipe
is let in ¾ in.

Front
clamp

Douglas Fir Workbench

To minimize costs, the author milled workbench stock from Douglas fir framing lumber, sawing clear sections from the center of 2x10s and 2x12s. The bench is fastened with drywall screws and lag bolts. Six pipe clamps in different configurations are used as vises.

OAK BLOCKS SPAN TAIL-VISE CLAMPS. The screw ends of the pipe clamps are screwed to the end of the bench through holes drilled in the clamp faces.

PIPES REST ON BLOCKS THAT TURN. Tail-vise pipe clamps are supported by blocks fastened with one screw. To slide a clamp past, turn the block.

FRONT CLAMPS ARE EASY TO ADJUST. The clamps fit in to holes in the bench front and are secured with large washers and speed pins.

Planing Beam Slides on Pipes

On the front of the bench is an adjustable, T-shaped planing beam that runs the full length of the bench. It is supported on both ends by the sliding tailpieces of Pony pipe clamps. The ½-in. cast-iron pipes on which the clamps slide are incorporated into the bench's legs. I used Pony clamps throughout this project because they are well made and slide and lock very smoothly.

The planing beam continuously supports the full length of a board standing on edge. The stock for the planing beam can be as narrow as 2 in. and as wide as 30 in. The planing beam can be set to any position in seconds. Of all of the bench's features, the planing beam is the most useful. I use it dozens of times daily when building a piece of furniture.

You've probably noticed that there is no front vise to secure the board being planed. Instead, the force of the plane pushes the workpiece into a tapered planing wedge attached to the far left end of the bench. This is an ancient device, and for handplaning it is far more practical than any vise. You can flip the board end for end or turn the other edge up in an instant with one hand. You don't even have to put down your plane.

To make a shoulder vise when needed, I drilled holes 6 in. on-center along the bench's front rail to mount pipe clamps horizontally. I pair up two clamps with a drop-in vise jaw, which is just a length of 1¾-in. square hardwood. The jaw can be as short as 8 in. or longer than 6 ft. I have several jaws of different lengths.

The front vise can be used with the planing beam supporting the workpiece from below. This is useful because some procedures, such as chopping mortises, drive the work downward through the jaws of a conventional vise, scarring the wood.

SLIDING HEIGHT ADJUSTMENT.
Pipe-clamp tailpieces slide on
cast-iron pipes held captive in
the top and bottom of the bench.
A T-shaped Douglas fir planing
beam rides on the clamps.

Traditional Tail Vise Is Replaced with Pipe Clamps

On the bench's top, two pipe-clamp bars
are recessed into a 10-in.-wide well, replacing a conventional tail vise and bench dogs.
The clamp-tightening screws project from
the right end of the bench, and the movable
jaws project ¾ in. above the top. Both the
fixed and movable jaws have oak faces. This
clamp setup makes it easy to hold down
boards for surface planing because nothing
projects above the board's surface to foul
the tool. The top clamp bars have a clamping capacity of just over 7 ft.

Blocks of wood support the pipes. Each
one is screwed to the frame of the bench
with a drywall screw. The single screw
allows each block to swing out of the way
of the pipe-clamp tailpieces as they are slid
to accommodate long work.

The top pipe clamps can also be used to
hold panels in place that have other tools
permanently attached, such as a vise or an
electric grinder. I have a tilting drill-press
vise attached to a square of medium-density
fiberboard (MDF) that I clamp to the
bench for metalworking or for holding a
piece of wood to be carved. I plan to design

a drop-in router table for the bench; there's enough space between the pipe-clamp bars to fit a small machine.

When the top clamps aren't in use, the well is covered by several sections of ¾-in. MDF that simply drop in and lie on top of the pipes. Because MDF is so inexpensive, I treat the panels as sacrificial surfaces. I cut into them, screw jigs to them, whack them with a hammer, and when they get too chewed up, I toss them. To save my back, I buy precut MDF meant for shelving; it comes either 12 in. or 16 in. wide. This precut stock is useful for all manner of jigs and prototypes, and I always have a few lengths around the shop.

Douglas Fir Makes a Solid Bench

The bench, as I built it, is 8 ft. long and was designed to accommodate fairly large work, such as doors and other architectural mill-work. The design can be shortened or lengthened, and it could be reversed end for end if you are left-handed.

PLANING WEDGE. When used with the planing beam, long work is held against a wedge-shaped stop at the end of the bench. The harder you push against the work, the more tightly it is held in place.

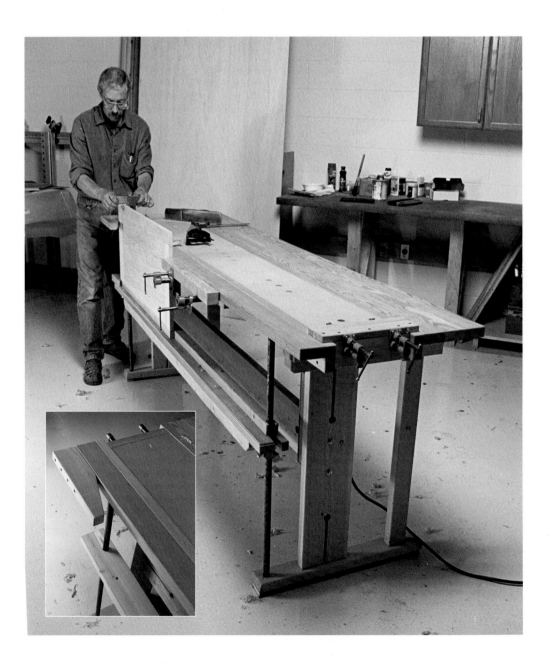

I built the bench out of Douglas fir instead of hardwood. Douglas fir at its best is a dense, stable wood that machines cleanly and holds fasteners well, which are important attributes given the way I wanted to assemble the bench.

Wide planks—2x10s and 2x12s—of Douglas fir framing lumber will often be sawn right out of the center of the log, and a half or more of the board will be quarter-sawn and knot free, with tight, straight grain. By carefully choosing and ripping these planks, you can get some beautiful material for a lot less than the price of even mediocre furniture woods. Some of the trimmed-out wood that isn't good enough for the bench can still be used for other projects such as shelves or sawhorses.

If you start with green lumber, sticker it for a few months to get the moisture content down. To prevent checking, trim the ends to get a clean surface and then apply duct tape over the end grain. Even if you start with kiln-dried wood, give it a couple of weeks indoors to stabilize before starting to cut. Use the best wood for the frame, benchtop, and beam, saving lesser-quality stock for the leg assembly.

Screw Joinery Is Fast and Strong

My method of assembling the bench with drywall screws and lag screws (and no fitted-and-glued joinery) is unconventional, but I've used this style of construction for years.

HORIZONTAL CLAMPS RUN FULL LENGTH. A pair of pipe clamps, running under the benchtop, hold work in the same way that a traditional tail vise does.

2¼ in. deep. The deep bore minimizes the amount of wood under the screw head, which in turn minimizes the loosening of the joint as the stock shrinks.

After drilling the counterbore, follow up with a long bit to drill a clearance hole for the screw shank. Then line up the pieces to be joined and install the screws a couple of turns to mark the centers, drill pilot holes at the marks in the adjoining piece and assemble the bench.

One of the advantages of this type of construction is that if the wood shrinks and the joints loosen up, you can retighten everything in a few minutes with a screwdriver. I did this about a month after assembling the bench, and it has stayed solid ever since. Don't overtighten the screws. Excessively crushing the wood under the screw's head ruins the resilience that allows a joint to flex slightly and remain tight.

The keyhole slots in the legs and stretcher are functional; as the boards shrink, they allow the wood to flex without cracking. In effect, they are preemptive cracks that look a lot better than the ones that would form randomly otherwise. When you install the lag bolts, drill clearance and pilot holes and go easy on the torque when you tighten them up. The joint will be stronger if you don't overstress the threads in the stretcher's end grain.

The pipes used with the clamps cut easily with a hacksaw or a small pipe cutter. For the smoothest operation of the clamps, clean up any burrs along the length of each pipe with a file and then smooth it down with emery paper. This is a messy operation, creating a staining black dust, so do it away from your woodworking area. Wipe down each pipe with a rag and paint thinner when you are done.

JOHN WHITE keeps the *Fine Woodworking* shop at The Taunton Press running smoothly.

The finished bench is rock solid, and the joinery goes quickly.

Most of the screws were counterbored with a ⅜-in. drill, sometimes quite deeply, to bring the screw heads ¾ in. shy of the edge being joined. On the 3-in.-wide, edge-jointed benchtop boards, the counterbore is

A Bench Built to Last

BY DICK McDONOUGH

If this workbench played football, I'm certain it would be a lineman. Because like the guards and tackles found on the gridiron, my bench is big and solid. And I wouldn't have it any other way.

Most of my work involves the fabrication of large case goods—entertainment centers, bookcases, and other types of storage furniture. And although much of the machine work gets done using a tablesaw and router, I still do a good deal of work at the bench. So when it was time to replace my older, smallish, and somewhat rickety workbench, I opted to make a new one with all the bells and whistles. The bench would provide plenty of size and sturdiness. Sturdiness is the operative word here. Indeed, no matter how aggressive I get with a saw, a handplane, or a mallet and chisel, the bench doesn't wobble. The result is a workbench that has just about everything I need.

The supersized top is another important feature. With about 22 sq. ft. of surface area, the top is great for supporting long boards and wide sheet goods. Two end vises, a front vise and a shoulder vise, along with a small army of benchdog holes, make it easy to secure almost any size stock to the bench.

My bench is considered left-handed, based on the location of the shoulder vise. If you prefer a right-handed bench, just build the shoulder vise on the right side.

The Base Creates a Sturdy Foundation

The bench owes much of its sturdiness to the design of the base. Yet its construction is pretty straightforward. It has just five main parts: three support frames and a pair of boxes. Screwing the frames and boxes together creates a single, rock-solid unit that can accept almost any kind of top. And the two boxes provide a ton of space for adding cabinets or drawers.

The center and right-side support frames are identical. But to provide additional support for the shoulder vise, the left-side support frame is longer and has an extra leg. I added seven heavy-duty levelers—one under each leg of the support frame.

To simplify the construction of the base, I made both plywood boxes the same size. They fit snugly between the top rail and the foot of the frames, which adds rigidity to the base.

If you include drawers in one of the boxes, cut the dadoes for the drawer-support cleats, and glue the cleats into the dadoes before the box is assembled.

Once the support frames and boxes were put together, I was able to assemble the base without much fuss. The boxes butt against the legs, with the bottom of the boxes simply resting on the narrow lip along the length of the foot. Attaching the boxes to the frames was a matter of driving five wood screws through the inside of the box and into each of the legs.

Once the base was built, I moved it to its final location. Next I leveled the top sur-face using winding sticks and the seven levelers. Then I was ready to build the top right on the base.

The Top Is Flat and Durable

The top has three main parts. There's a center section made from veneered particleboard. Attached to the center section are two 6-in.-wide edgings—one in front, the other in back—and both made from glued-up solid maple.

Start with the center section To help keep costs under control, I face-glued three pieces of particleboard together—a ⅝-in.-thick piece sandwiched between two ¾-in.-thick pieces.

A Variety of Vises and Ample Storage

SHOULDER VISE ADDS CLAMPING OPTIONS. The lack of a vise screw between the jaw surfaces makes the shoulder vise especially handy when a board must be clamped vertically.

FRONT VISE IS NICE. Used in conjunction with round benchdogs, the front vise lets the author work comfortably from the end of the bench.

DRAWERS GALORE. The shallow top drawer provides a perfect place for the author to store his favorite chisels.

First, I joined one of the ¾-in.-thick
pieces to the ⅝-in.-thick piece, making sure
all of the edges were flush. Then, I used a
⅝-in.-dia. core-box bit to cut three ⅝-in.-
deep grooves across the underside of the
⅝-in.-thick particleboard. When the remaining piece of particleboard was added, the
groove produced a ⅝-in. semicircular hole,
which accommodated a threaded rod that
helps secure the solid-maple edgings.

A workbench top gets a lot of wear and
tear, so I used a ³⁄₁₆-in.-thick veneer on top.
And to make sure any movement stresses
would be equal, I also veneered the bottom.

To make the veneer, I resawed maple to
about a ⁵⁄₁₆-in. thickness on the bandsaw. I
used a thickness planer to bring the material
to final thickness. Then I jointed one edge
of each piece of veneer and ripped the
other edge parallel on the tablesaw.

At this point, the veneer was ready to be
applied to the particleboard. But faced with
having to veneer such a large surface with
thick veneer and without a lot of clamps,
I used a somewhat unusual gluing-and-
clamping technique (see pp. 82–83).

A MASSIVE TOP ON A STURDY MODULAR BASE

To help keep costs under control, the top is a hybrid,
a mix of solid maple, thick veneer, and particleboard.
The base construction is surprisingly simple—a pair
of plywood boxes sandwiched between three
frames—yet the single unit that results is as solid
as a '72 Buick.

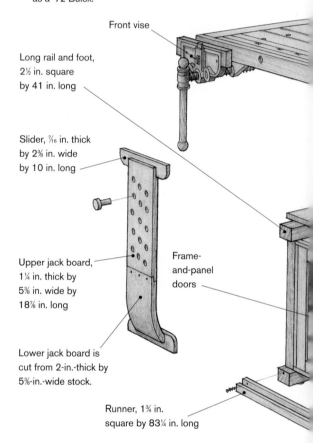

Front vise

Long rail and foot,
2½ in. square
by 41 in. long

Slider, ⁷⁄₁₆ in. thick
by 2⅜ in. wide
by 10 in. long

Upper jack board,
1¼ in. thick by
5⅜ in. wide by
18⅞ in. long

Frame-
and-panel
doors

Lower jack board is
cut from 2-in.-thick by
5⅜-in.-wide stock.

Runner, 1¾ in.
square by 83¼ in. long

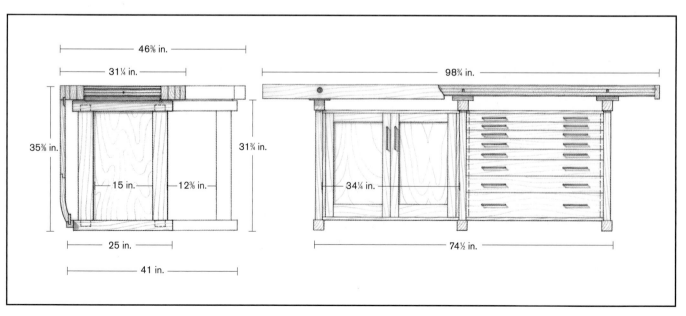

46⅝ in.

31¼ in.

35⅝ in.

31¾ in.

15 in.

12⅜ in.

25 in.

41 in.

98¾ in.

34¼ in.

74½ in.

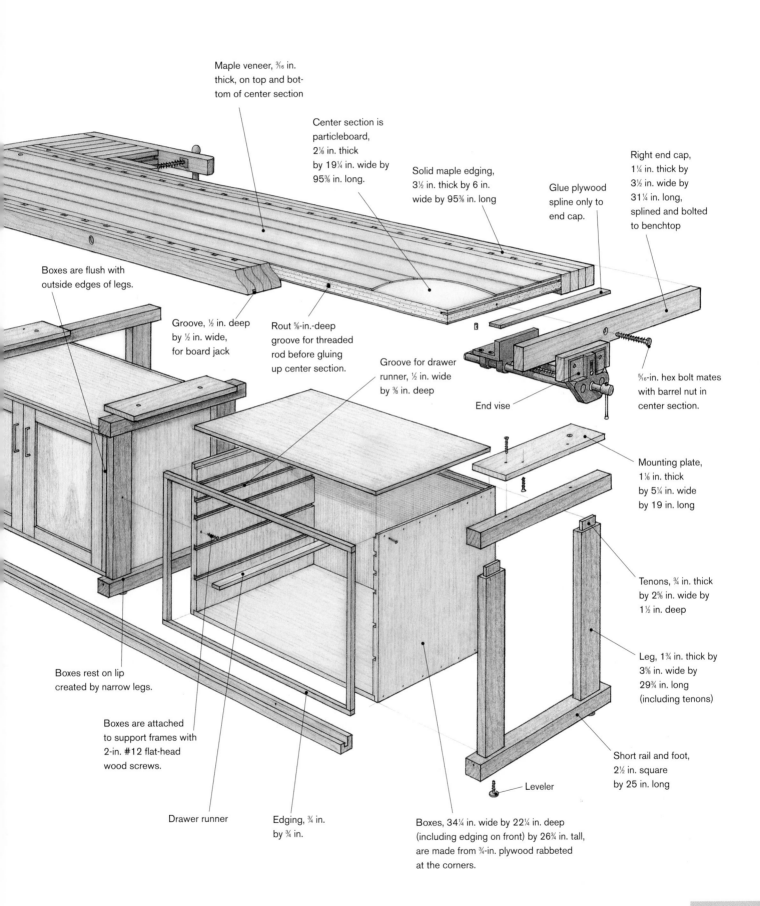

Maple veneer, ³⁄₁₆ in. thick, on top and bottom of center section

Center section is particleboard, 2⅛ in. thick by 19¼ in. wide by 95⅝ in. long.

Solid maple edging, 3½ in. thick by 6 in. wide by 95⅝ in. long

Glue plywood spline only to end cap.

Right end cap, 1¼ in. thick by 3½ in. wide by 31¼ in. long, splined and bolted to benchtop

Boxes are flush with outside edges of legs.

Groove, ½ in. deep by ½ in. wide, for board jack

Rout ⅝-in.-deep groove for threaded rod before gluing up center section.

Groove for drawer runner, ½ in. wide by ⅜ in. deep

⁵⁄₁₆-in. hex bolt mates with barrel nut in center section.

End vise

Mounting plate, 1⅛ in. thick by 5¼ in. wide by 19 in. long

Boxes rest on lip created by narrow legs.

Tenons, ¾ in. thick by 2⅝ in. wide by 1½ in. deep

Leg, 1¾ in. thick by 3⅝ in. wide by 29¾ in. long (including tenons)

Boxes are attached to support frames with 2-in. #12 flat-head wood screws.

Drawer runner

Edging, ¾ in. by ¾ in.

Boxes, 34¼ in. wide by 22¼ in. deep (including edging on front) by 26¾ in. tall, are made from ¾-in. plywood rabbeted at the corners.

Leveler

Short rail and foot, 2½ in. square by 25 in. long

Gluing Thick Veneer to a Large Surface

Large surfaces, like the top of my bench, are a challenge to veneer because it's difficult to get good clamping pressure over the entire surface. I have enough clamps for most jobs but nowhere near the number I'd need for my jumbo-sized benchtop. And new clamps don't come cheap.

The answer proved to be a set of 10 shopmade clamping cauls. And because I was able to use mostly scrap wood, the total cost was under $12★—less than I'd pay for a single commercial clamp.

It's easy to make these clamps. The top "jaw" is a 24-in. length of 4¾-in.-wide medium-density fiberboard (MDF) screwed to a 24-in.-long 2x3. The bottom jaw is a 24-in.-long 2x4. To prevent the MDF surfaces

from ending up glued to the veneer, add a healthy coat of paste wax to each one. The ends of the jaws accept a 9-in.-long, ⅜-in.-dia. threaded rod that is fitted with a washer and nut on both ends.

To begin veneering, spread a generous coat of yellow glue on the mating surfaces of the veneer and particleboard. A short painter's roller allows you to spread the glue easily and quickly. When working with a large surface area, it's important to have a good assembly game-plan worked out because yellow glue can start to tack up in less than 10 minutes. You need to get the glue down and the clamps tightened up without delay.

Place the veneer glue-side down on the particleboard. Butt the pieces together, but don't add glue to

CLAMP THE VENEER TO THE PARTICLEBOARD WITH CLAMPING CAULS. No need to have a small fortune in clamps to do this glue-up. Shopmade clamping cauls get the job done for pennies.

the edges or worry about a perfect joint quite yet. Let the veneer overhang the particleboard all around.

Then start clamping down the veneer. To help avoid lengthwise buckling, tighten the clamps at one end and work toward the other.

Both the top and bottom surfaces of the particleboard must be veneered; if only the top is veneered, it can create uneven stresses that can cause the top to cup.

Once both sides have been veneered, true up the edge joints with a router equipped with a ⅜-in.-dia. straight bit. Use a long piece of stock as a straightedge and rout a ³⁄₁₆-in.-deep groove centered along the entire length of each joint line. Then use the clamping cauls to glue ⅜-in.-wide by ³⁄₁₆-in.-thick inlays into the grooves. This technique results in near-perfect edge joints.

INLAYS CONCEAL IMPERFECT VENEER JOINTS

ROUT THE JOINT. To clean up any gaps, a router and edge guide are used to cut a shallow groove centered on the long joint.

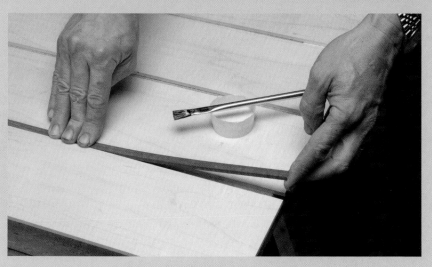

ADD THE INLAY. Thin strips of cherry fill in the grooves, producing tight joint lines along the full length of the bench.

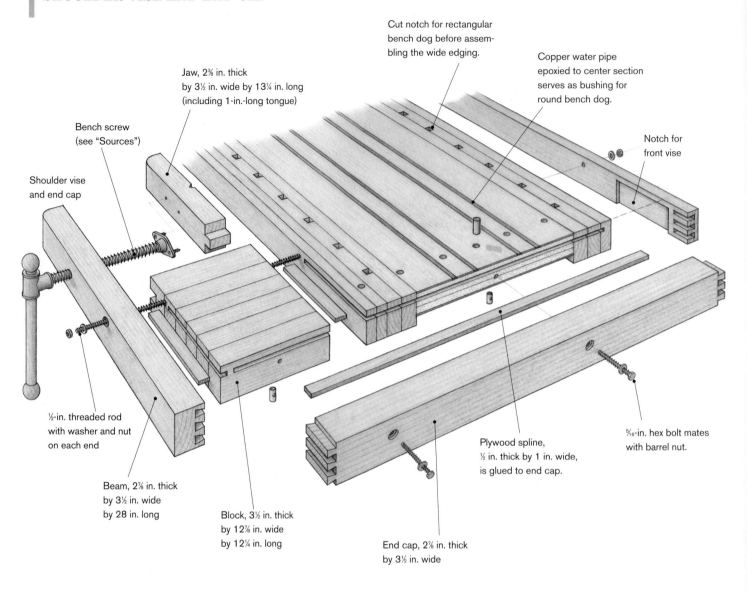

Cut notch for rectangular bench dog before assembling the wide edging.

Copper water pipe epoxied to center section serves as bushing for round bench dog.

Jaw, 2⅜ in. thick by 3½ in. wide by 13¼ in. long (including 1-in.-long tongue)

Bench screw (see "Sources")

Notch for front vise

Shoulder vise and end cap

½-in. threaded rod with washer and nut on each end

Beam, 2⅞ in. thick by 3½ in. wide by 28 in. long

Block, 3½ in. thick by 12⅞ in. wide by 12¼ in. long

Plywood spline, ½ in. thick by 1 in. wide, is glued to end cap.

⅝₆-in. hex bolt mates with barrel nut.

End cap, 2⅞ in. thick by 3½ in. wide

Sources

Many of the tools and accessories mentioned in this chapter can be found at www.wood-craft.com.

Wide edgings accept bench dogs The wide edgings that run along the front and back of the bench are made of solid maple. That way the bench dogs have plenty of support when in use.

I routed the dadoes that create the openings for the rectangular-shaped bench dogs before the pieces were glued together.

I also wanted bench dogs to work with the front vise. But it was going to be a hassle to chop out all of those square mortises with a chisel. Plus, the particleboard wouldn't

hold up well when the dogs got squeezed. So I opted to use round bench dogs. That way I simply had to bore a hole to accept it. And to reinforce the particleboard, I glued a short length of ¾-in. copper water pipe into the hole.

Three lengths of ½-in.-dia. threaded rod, with a washer and nut on each end, secure the wide, solid-maple edgings to the veneered center section. The rods extend through the "holes" in the particleboard and into through-holes in the edgings.

To drill the through-holes, I first cut each piece of edging to final length. Then to mark the location of the holes in the edgings, I clamped one piece to the center section. I made a center-point marker by driving a finish nail in the end of a long, ½-in.-dia. dowel. The nail must be centered in the end. I ran the dowel through the holes in the particleboard and used the nail to mark the center point of the hole in the edging. Once all of the points were marked, I drilled all of the holes through each piece of edging.

The threaded rod closest to the left end is longer than the other two rods because it extends all the way through the shoulder-vise parts. I used the same technique to mark the center points on the shoulder-vise parts.

I then face-glued the edgings and glued and clamped them to the front and back of the bench.

The space under the bench is put to use

Those big boxes in the base provide plenty of storage space. I placed eight drawers in the right-hand box. Plus, to take advantage of the space between the top of the box and the underside of the benchtop, I added a shallow through-drawer that extends from front to back, with a face on each end of the drawer, so it can be accessed from both sides of the workbench.

The left-hand box holds the parts of a project I'm building. The box includes a hinged shelf that pivots up and out of the way when it's not needed. The frame-and-panel doors keep dust from filling up the box.

Board jacks support long stock The board jacks (one in front and one in back) are handy additions to the bench. When a board is clamped in the front, or shoulder, vise, the jack holds up the unsupported

end. To accommodate boards of varying length, the jack is able to slide along the full length of the bench.

Power strips bring the juice Because my bench is several feet from a wall, I added power strips along the front and back edges, making it easier to use power tools at the bench.

The bench has been serving me well for several years now. During that time, it has picked up plenty of scratches and dents, but it's as solid as ever. And I expect it's going to stay that way for many years to come.

★ *Please note that price estimates are from 2001.*

DICK McDONOUGH lives in Flint, Michigan, where he's a full-time finish carpenter and part-time wood-working teacher.

Rock-Solid Workbench

BY JON LEPPO

I knew that when I eventually got around to building my dream workbench, it would have to meet a few basic requirements. It would have to be sturdy enough to last a few lifetimes. It would have to have storage underneath. And it would have to have good front and end vises so that I wouldn't have to do a lot to get a workpiece held securely.

In 1998, I finally built my bench. And I'm pleased to say that after years of heavy work, it has fulfilled my expectations, and then some. It's rock-solid and has plenty of useful storage, thanks to 15 drawers and an area of open space between the base and the top.

Building such a large workbench can be an intimidating task, but it's actually basic woodworking. The only part of the bench that calls for anything other than straightforward biscuit and mortise-and-tenon joinery is the end vise. Whether you decide to build this bench using the plans that follow or add the end vise to a bench you already have, this chapter walks you through the process.

Vises, Bench Dogs, and a Board Jack Help Anchor Workpieces

The front and end vises, along with bench dogs and a board jack, offer plenty of clamping options.

In the front of the bench I had planned to use a typical cast-iron vise with wood jaws until I ran across an Internet ad for a used patternmaker's vise, and I couldn't resist the temptation to buy. The vise, built in the 1930s by the Emmert Manufacturing Co., allows me to clamp a workpiece in almost any position. Patternmakers favor this type of vise because it adjusts in several planes, making it possible to hold work of almost any shape. Like me, you'll occasionally see a used Emmert vise offered for sale on the Internet.

Also, you can sometimes find them at vintage tool dealers or, more rarely, at flea markets. Expect to pay upwards of $500★ for one in good condition.

My vise is one of the larger ones Emmert produced. Modern reproductions of the vise are available in mostly smaller sizes, generally about 15 in. long. Some of these are fairly inexpensive, about $300★, and the quality is decent. Higher-quality ones can cost more than $1,000★.

A sliding board jack helps support long, wide stock, with the front end of the stock held in the Emmert vise. The board jack is adapted directly from one I found in *The Workbench Book* by Scott Landis (The Taunton Press, 1987), modified only slightly to fit my bench. The bottom track screws to

the bottom frame, capturing the board jack. An occasional application of paste wax to the tracks keeps the jack sliding smoothly.

End Vise Adds Versatility

I originally considered a commercially made twin-screw end vise, but in the end the extra versatility that a traditional vise offers has made the effort worthwhile. Whether you build my bench from the ground up or not, adding an end vise to a workbench will make it much more user-friendly. Building the end vise is also the trickiest part of the process.

The end-vise hardware consists of four parts (the vise hardware is available from Woodcraft—www.woodcraft.com): a main plate that includes a cylindrical nut; a long screw with a flanged bracket and handle collar; a top guide plate with a lengthwise groove and a pair of threaded bolt holes;

and a bottom guide plate with a corresponding groove and a pair of countersunk through-holes. A pair of bolts is also included. By the way, it's important to have the hardware on hand before making the vise. Some of the dimensions are taken directly off the steel parts.

The main plate is screwed to the edge of the benchtop. All of the other parts, effectively working as one component, simply slide along the main plate. One end of the long screw is attached to the outside end of the vise, while the other end is threaded into the nut on the main plate. As the screw is turned, it threads in or out of the fixed nut, and in the process the vise is carried along for the ride. The top and bottom guide plates connect the vise and the main plate while allowing the vise to slide. The secret here is the single lengthwise groove near one edge of each guide plate. The

The base of this bench, modeled after the one master woodworker Robert Whitley built for his bench, consists of five frame-and-panel assemblies—two end frames, a back frame and two horizontal frames—bolted together with carriage bolts. And while I wouldn't exactly call this a knockdown bench, it can be disassembled.

I joined the panel frames with a double row of #20 biscuits, mostly because of speed and convenience. The base carcase sees mostly compression loads on vertical grain members rather than racking forces, which would stress the biscuit joints. A purist would have used mortises and tenons here. But I've had no trouble using biscuits in this kind of application.

The top is made from hard-maple laminations face-glued together. Each end of the bench has a long tenon. Later, when a pair of caps is made, each tenon fits into a mortise in the corresponding cap pieces.

I used a circular saw to cut the tenons. With a straight-edge clamped to the benchtop to guide the saw, I made several crosscut kerfs and chiseled away the waste.

Both the long and short end caps are mortised to accept the tenons on each end of the bench.

To allow the top to move, the end caps aren't glued in place. Instead, each one is held in place with a pair of bolts. One of the bolt holes on each end cap is slotted so that it can move with the top. Once I had the end caps mounted, I flattened the entire benchtop using handplanes and winding sticks. Mounting an Emmert vise is relatively simple, although they are often heavy (mine is about 85 lbs.). The vise itself mounts on a large hinge that's mortised into the top face of the benchtop and also the front face of the front apron. To allow clearance for the vise screw, a channel is cut into the underside of the apron and the benchtop.

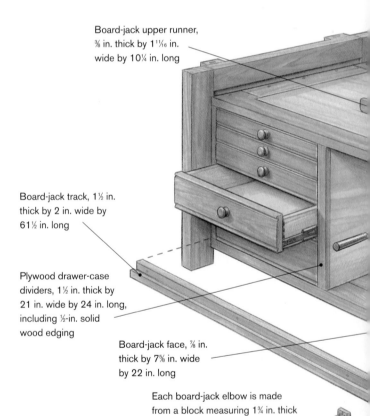

Long end cap, 3¼ in. thick by 4 in. wide by 33⅜ in. long

Main top, 2⅜ in. thick by 96½ in. long, including 1-in.-long tenons

Front apron, 1⅝ in. thick by 4 in. wide by 80⅛ in. long

Board-jack upper runner, ⅜ in. thick by 1¹¹⁄₁₆ in. wide by 10¼ in. long

Board-jack track, 1½ in. thick by 2 in. wide by 61½ in. long

Plywood drawer-case dividers, 1½ in. thick by 21 in. wide by 24 in. long, including ½-in. solid wood edging

Board-jack face, ⅞ in. thick by 7⅝ in. wide by 22 in. long

Each board-jack elbow is made from a block measuring 1¾ in. thick by 2¼ in. wide by 6 in. long

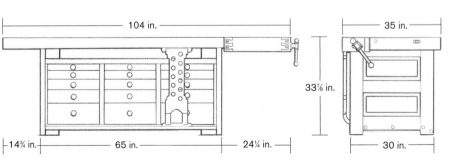

104 in.

35 in.

33⅞ in.

14¾ in.

65 in.

24¼ in.

30 in.

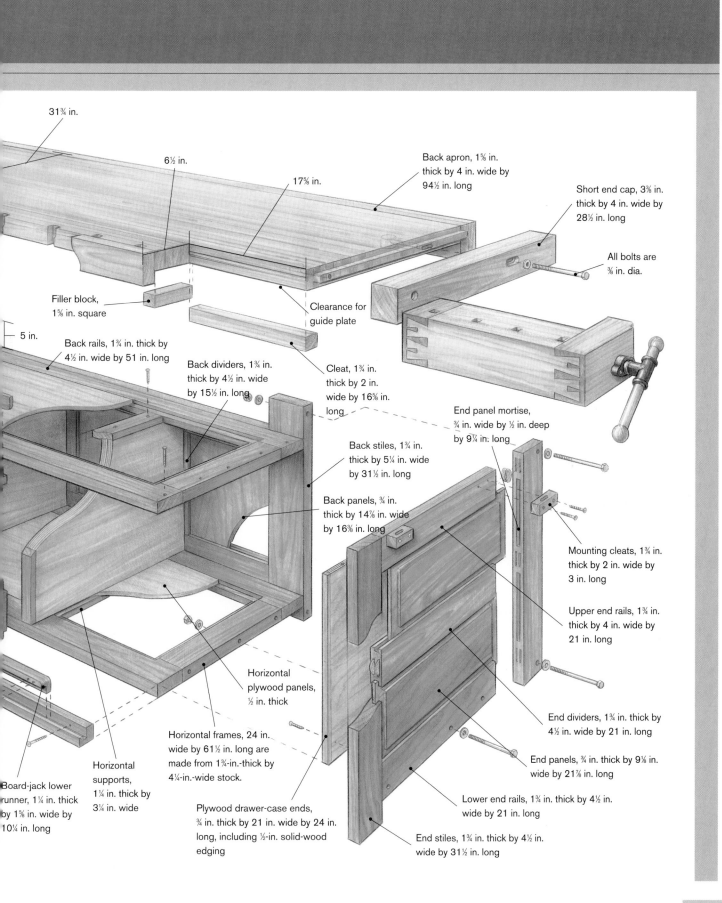

31¾ in.

6½ in.

17⅝ in.

Back apron, 1⅝ in. thick by 4 in. wide by 94½ in. long

Short end cap, 3⅜ in. thick by 4 in. wide by 28½ in. long

All bolts are ⅜ in. dia.

Filler block, 1⅝ in. square

Clearance for guide plate

5 in.

Back rails, 1¾ in. thick by 4½ in. wide by 51 in. long

Back dividers, 1¾ in. thick by 4½ in. wide by 15½ in. long

Cleat, 1¾ in. thick by 2 in. wide by 16⅝ in. long

End panel mortise, ¾ in. wide by ½ in. deep by 9¼ in. long

Back stiles, 1¾ in. thick by 5¼ in. wide by 31½ in. long

Back panels, ¾ in. thick by 14⅞ in. wide by 16⅝ in. long

Mounting cleats, 1¾ in. thick by 2 in. wide by 3 in. long

Upper end rails, 1¾ in. thick by 4 in. wide by 21 in. long

Horizontal plywood panels, ½ in. thick

Horizontal frames, 24 in. wide by 61½ in. long are made from 1¾-in.-thick by 4¼-in.-wide stock.

Horizontal supports, 1¼ in. thick by 3¼ in. wide

Board-jack lower runner, 1¼ in. thick by 1⅝ in. wide by 10¼ in. long

Plywood drawer-case ends, ¾ in. thick by 21 in. wide by 24 in. long, including ½-in. solid-wood edging

End dividers, 1¾ in. thick by 4½ in. wide by 21 in. long

End panels, ¾ in. thick by 9⅛ in. wide by 21⅞ in. long

Lower end rails, 1¾ in. thick by 4½ in. wide by 21 in. long

End stiles, 1¾ in. thick by 4½ in. wide by 31½ in. long

grooves in the guide plates simply slide over the main plate, held apart by the wooden core.

Core prevents a sloppy fit The core maintains the correct distance between the top and bottom guide plates.

To make the core, start by measuring between the top and bottom guide plates while the two parts are assembled to the main plate. Add 1/64 in. or so for clearance, then rip the core to width. Now clamp the two guide plates to the core and try sliding the core along the main plate. If the fit is too loose, remove the plates, then run the core through a thickness planer, but make the cut an especially thin one. Repeat as needed. If the fit is too tight, add shim stock between the core and a guide plate.

Cut the core to length and drill a clearance hole for the vise screw in one end. Then hollow out the center of the core using a Forstner bit, and clean up what remains with a chisel. Now use the top guide plate to mark the locations of the

mounting holes on each end of the vise. The end of the plate should be flush with the drilled end of the core. To provide a little clearance between the core and the main plate, the slot in the guide plate should extend past the edge of the core by no more than about 1/32 in. Once marked, use a drill press to bore the holes.

Cut and assemble the end-vise parts
After cutting the front, end, top, jaw and dog-hole block to size, it's time to tackle the double dovetails that join the front to the end and the jaw. Double dovetails simply are small dovetails cut between larger ones (see the top photos on p. 92). They require a lot of chopping by hand, even after hogging out much of the waste with Forstner bits. Plus, it takes special care to avoid breaking the pins at the narrow end.

Mark the tails on each end of the front, then use a backsaw to remove a good part of the waste. Finish the work with a chisel. Now mark the pin profile. I clamped the jaw on end in the Emmert vise and used a

A Vise With Good Moves

The jaws on an Emmert patternmaker's vise adjust in three planes, a feature that can prove useful when clamping odd-shaped parts. The jaws rotate 360 (left), pivot 90 (center), and taper (right).

End-Vise Construction

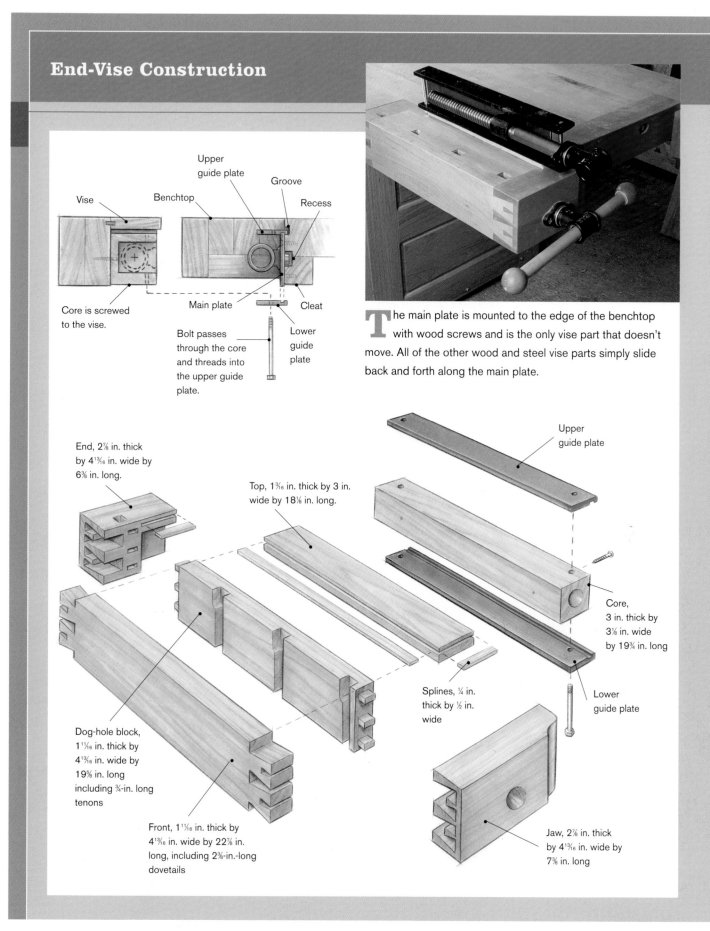

Vise

Benchtop

Upper guide plate

Groove

Recess

Core is screwed to the vise.

Main plate

Cleat

Bolt passes through the core and threads into the upper guide plate.

Lower guide plate

The main plate is mounted to the edge of the benchtop with wood screws and is the only vise part that doesn't move. All of the other wood and steel vise parts simply slide back and forth along the main plate.

End, 2⅞ in. thick by 4¹³⁄₁₆ in. wide by 6⅜ in. long.

Top, 1³⁄₁₆ in. thick by 3 in. wide by 18⅛ in. long.

Upper guide plate

Core, 3 in. thick by 3⅛ in. wide by 19¾ in. long

Dog-hole block, 1¹¹⁄₁₆ in. thick by 4¹³⁄₁₆ in. wide by 19⅝ in. long including ¾-in. long tenons

Front, 1¹¹⁄₁₆ in. thick by 4¹³⁄₁₆ in. wide by 22⅞ in. long, including 2⅜-in.-long dovetails

Splines, ¼ in. thick by ½ in. wide

Lower guide plate

Jaw, 2⅞ in. thick by 4¹³⁄₁₆ in. wide by 7⅞ in. long

DOVETAILING THE END CAPS AND FRONT OF THE VISE

CUT THE DOVETAILS. Use a fine-toothed backsaw to cut the sides of the dovetails.

MARK THE PIN LOCATIONS ON THE OUTSIDE AND INSIDE ENDS. With the end cap clamped in a vise, the front piece is used as a template to mark the pin locations.

CUT THE PINS. Use a Forstner bit to remove most of the waste material from the pin ends. A chisel takes care of any waste that remains.

ASSEMBLING THE VISE

BEGIN GLUING THE VISE PARTS. Glue the end, the jaw, the dog-hole block and the top. You'll need several clamps to squeeze the four parts together.

ADD THE FRONT PIECE. Apply glue to the tails on the front piece and the pins on the end and jaw, then use a mallet to tap the front into place.

MAKING THE CORE

THE CORE CONNECTS THE VISE TO THE HARDWARE

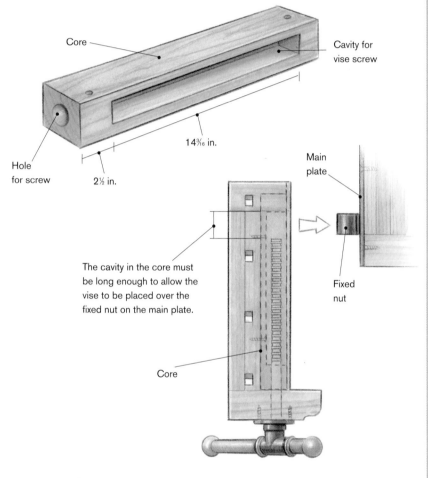

Core

Cavity for vise screw

Hole for screw

14³⁄₁₆ in.

2½ in.

The cavity in the core must be long enough to allow the vise to be placed over the fixed nut on the main plate.

Main plate

Fixed nut

Core

Cavity for vise screw

Core

⅜ in.

3⅛ in.

2 in.

¾ in.

2⅝ in.

Guide plate

Size the core to fit precisely between the upper and lower guide plates.

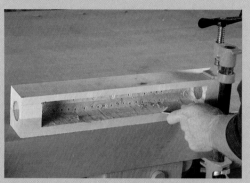

THE CORE PROVIDES A MEANS TO SECURE THE VISE HARDWARE. The core is made from a glued-up block of wood. After drilling out the cavity, use a chisel to clean up any waste that remains.

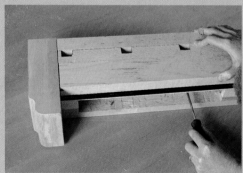

MOUNTING THE CORE. With the upper guide plate temporarily placed on the core to serve as a spacer, slip the core and plate into the vise cavity (top). Then attach the core to the vise by driving four screws through the core and into the dog-hole block (bottom).

Installing the End Vise

SECURE THE MAIN PLATE. Position the top edge of the plate slightly above the bottom edge of the groove in the top.

SLIDE THE TOP PLATE ONTO THE MAIN PLATE. When properly located, the top guide plate should slide smoothly along the main plate without interference.

chisel to mark most of the pin profile, reaching places my marking knife couldn't. Remove the pin waste using the drill press. You can do this with Forstner bits and then finish with a chisel. Repeat the steps to cut the pins on the end piece.

The dog-hole block has three tenons on each end that fit into mortises cut into the end and the jaw. Cut the dog holes first, then use a router to expand the top end slightly, creating a small step.

The top piece has a spline groove on three edges. Cut matching grooves in the end, the jaw and the dog-hole block.

After dry-fitting all of the parts to make sure everything goes together okay, glue and clamp the end, the jaw, the top and the dog-hole block. Then you can glue the front in place.

Mount the vise The entire vise hangs on the main plate that mounts at the notch in the right end of the top. But, before the vise can be mounted, you need to cut a groove in the edge of the top to provide clearance for the upper guide plate. A router and an edge guide, with the router operated horizontally, can be used to create most of the groove. A chisel is used to extend the groove to the corner of the notch.

Before the main plate can be mounted, a shallow hole must be drilled in the edge of the benchtop to provide clearance for the bolt head on the back of the plate. Finally, glue the cleat in place.

The top edge of the main plate must be parallel to the benchtop, and the front edge of the plate must be flush with the front of the end cap. It also must be located a dis-

MOUNT THE VISE. **With the cylindrical nut on the main plate roughly aligned with the open space at the back end of the core cavity, slip the vise onto the guide plate. Then thread the screw into the nut.**

BOLT THE GUIDE PLATES. **After slipping the lower guide plate onto the bottom edge of the main plate, add the two bolts that thread into tapped holes in the upper guide plate.**

tance from the benchtop that's equal to the thickness of the top plus the thickness of the top guide plate, minus the depth of the groove in the guide plate.

Once everything is lined up, drive a couple of screws to secure the main plate in place. The remaining screws will be installed after the vise has been test-fitted. Next, add the core. Temporarily place the top guide plate on the core and slide the two parts into the vise. While squeezing the plate between the core and the underside of the top, drive four screws through the back of the core and into the dog-hole block. Once the core has been installed, remove the plate. Now drill a hole in the jaw and slip the screw through the hole and into the core. A pair of screws driven through the flange secure the screw to the vise.

Next, with the top guide plate resting on the main plate, slip the vise over the guide plate. Position the vise so that the cylindrical nut ends up in the opening between the end of the screw and the back of the core.

To complete the vise assembly, insert the two bolts supplied with the hardware through holes drilled earlier in the core. Snug up each bolt with a few turns of an adjustable wrench. The wood handles are made from maple dowels, with ends made from hardwood balls that are available from a number of woodworking mail-order outfits.

★*Please note that price estimates are from 2003.*

JON LEPPO is an amateur woodworker in Denver, Colorado.

Build a Better Sawhorse

BY VOICU MARIAN

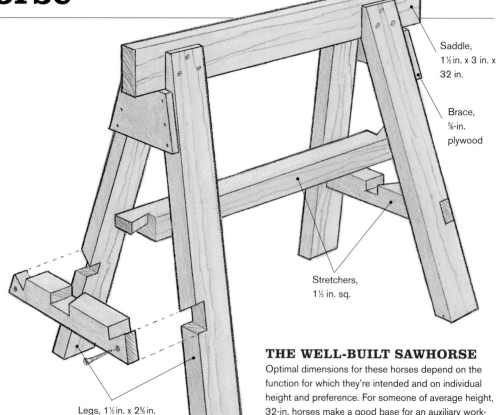

Saddle,
1½ in. x 3 in. x
32 in.

Brace,
⅝-in.
plywood

Stretchers,
1½ in. sq.

Legs, 1½ in. x 2⅝ in.

THE WELL-BUILT SAWHORSE
Optimal dimensions for these horses depend on the
function for which they're intended and on individual
height and preference. For someone of average height,
32-in. horses make a good base for an auxiliary workbench, and 24 in. horses are about right for an assembly and finishing platform.

I made my first pair of these sawhorses a
few years back while remodeling my
house because it was uncomfortable
working stooped down on the floor. With
a hollow core door on top, I had a fairly
sturdy workbench that could be moved
easily from one room to the next. After finishing up in the house, I took them back to
the shop, and that's where they have proven
their value.

My workbench always seems to be
cluttered with tools. Before I made these
horses, I often used the tablesaw as an auxiliary bench. That worked well as long as I
didn't need to cut anything.

Now I have a second workbench: A pair
of these sawhorses provides a strong, stable
base; a couple of thick, heavy planks atop
them form a perfectly serviceable benchtop; and a plank across the stretchers makes

a good shelf for bench planes and other larger tools that normally clutter a bench surface. I clamp horses and planks together for stability and use C-clamps and bar or pipe clamps in lieu of vises, dogs, and bench stops. When I'm finished with the bench, it disassembles and stores easily.

What makes these horses different from most, though, is the joinery. I first saw this half-lap, half-dovetail joint (see the drawing) used by an old carpenter when I was growing up in Romania. It's a strong joint, not too finicky to cut—especially in softwood. The joint gives these horses greater strength and rigidity, a much longer life and, as a bonus, a nice look. Also, the practice you gain in laying out and cutting the joinery in construction lumber will transfer to the fine work you do in hardwoods.

Construction Sequence

I dimension all my stock first and then bevel all the edges with a block plane. To ease assembly and ensure consistency, I nail together a quick, simple set-up jig, consisting of three pieces of scrapwood on a plywood base (see the photo).

I determine the angle of the legs by eye rather than by using any mathematical formula. I hold two legs upright and adjust their spread until it looks right. I then check with a protractor for future reference, and I read 35 degrees.

I cut the notches at the top of the legs for the saddle first, space the legs with a block the same size as the saddle, and then lay out the short end stretchers. I lay out and cut the half-lap first, scribing from the insides and outsides of the legs. I mark out the dovetails on the top side of the stretcher at 8 degrees, cut them, and scribe around them with a sharp pencil onto the legs (see the photo). I cut and chisel out the leg to receive the stretcher. When the joint is assembled, leg and stretcher should be flush.

With all four end assemblies complete, I stand up a pair at a time and install the sad-

A SIMPLE, NAILED-TOGETHER JIG SPEEDS LAYOUT **and ensures consistency from horse to horse. Here, the author scribes around the end stretcher dovetail to cut out its mortise in the leg.**

dle, leaving a 4-in. overhang at each end. This provides a wider support for the boards I use as a benchtop as well as clearance for my feet. For now, one screw holds it together. Next I adjust the sawhorse so it's square to the surface it's standing on. Then I place the long stretcher across the short ones. I center it and mark it for length and for the shoulder of the half-lap.

The rest of the process is the same as for the short stretchers, except I put the dovetails on opposite sides at each end. I do this more for aesthetics than for any structural reason. I glue the long stretcher in place and screw it from below. I then put two more screws on each side of the legs, for a total of three screws, into the saddle at the top of each leg.

The last thing I do is cut the tips of the feet, so they don't rock. To mark them, I lay the sole of my square flat on its side, scribe around each foot, and then saw them off.

VOICU MARIAN works wood in Alliance, Ohio.

Sawhorses
for the Shop

BY CHRISTIAN
BECKSVOORT

THREE HORSES THAT COVER all of your shop needs.

Sawhorses are an indispensable part of my shop equipment. No matter what the process or project, I reach for a horse to saw boards, to stand on, to lay out panels and joints, to hold parts, and to elevate cabinets for sanding or planing. I also use sawhorses for drill-press work supports, assembly, finishing, outdoor power carving and routing, changing lightbulbs and even photography. I've constructed a pair each of three different heights: 1 ft., 2 ft., and 3 ft. The 3-ft. set includes height extenders for even more versatility.

Sawhorses are not fine furniture. I built these horses quick and dirty, to be useful but sturdy. The material is whatever I happened to have on hand at the time: pine, ash, oak, fir, and even the ever- plentiful cherry scraps. For joinery I relied on butt joints held together with glue and screws. I spent a lot of time and effort on my toolbox and will do the same when I have to replace my aging workbench. But sawhorses are a different story. I give them the roughest treatment without a second thought. While studying and restoring Shaker pieces, I noticed that although most of their work reflects meticulous craftsmanship and graceful design, many of their tables, stands, and cases intended for shop use are merely glued and nailed together. They had the same idea.

Wide-Topped Short Horse Serves Two Purposes

My shortest sawhorse is really a larger version of a footstool or a small bench. It's about a foot tall and is assembled with screws. Because the top of this horse is relatively large, it has a handhold in the middle to make it easy to pick up the horse and move it with one hand.

Generally, I use the short horse for sawing long planks to rough length. If I'm cutting off just a couple of inches from the end of a long plank, a pair of these horses goes

STEPPING UP FOR CROSSCUTS.
The 1-ft.-tall horse raises the workpiece so that you can use a crosscut saw comfortably.

under the long section. If I'm cutting the plank near the middle, the sawcut is made between the horses to support the cutoff.

Most often I'll use the short horses to bring a case piece up to a comfortable working height. For example, I'm over 6 ft. tall, so a 30-in.-tall cabinet that needs to be planed or sanded is in a much better working position for me with this horse placed underneath it. When edging wide panels or case backs, I set one end into my bench vise and support the other end on the short horse. My ancient Skil® belt sander weighs close to 15 lbs., and I prefer to use it in the horizontal position. Consequently, when finish-sanding the top of a 5-ft.-tall cabinet, I stand on the short horse to make sanding easier. When working on a nearly completed piece, I pad the top of the horse with carpet scraps to protect the piece from unwanted dings, dents, and scratches. I'm not the only one who finds my short sawhorses useful. The short horse gives every photographer

WIDE-TOPPED SHORT HORSE

Essentially, this horse is a stool, but it can be used as a short bench for sawing, for holding tall work in a vise, and holding case work off the floor for finishing.

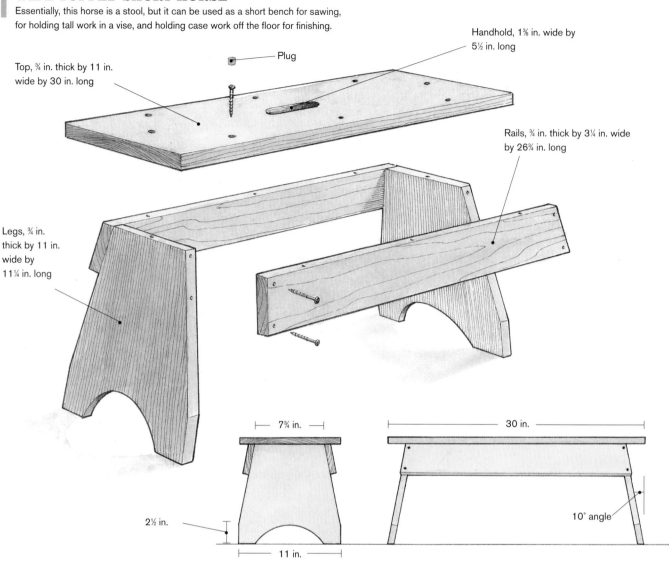

Plug

Handhold, 1⅜ in. wide by 5½ in. long

Top, ¾ in. thick by 11 in. wide by 30 in. long

Rails, ¾ in. thick by 3¼ in. wide by 26¾ in. long

Legs, ¾ in. thick by 11 in. wide by 11¼ in. long

7¾ in.

30 in.

2½ in.

10° angle

11 in.

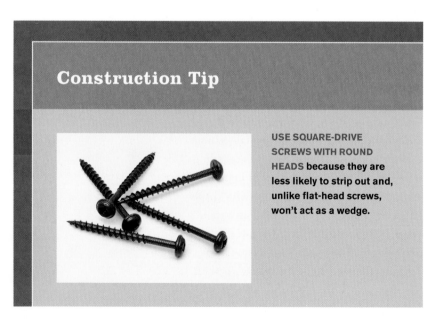

Construction Tip

USE SQUARE-DRIVE SCREWS WITH ROUND HEADS because they are less likely to strip out and, unlike flat-head screws, won't act as a wedge.

who comes into my shop a great view of the work in progress on my tall workbench.

The footprint of the base is the same size as the top so that the horse is safe to stand on, and a pair can be stacked. The legs are cut at 10 degrees along both sides and are tilted at the same angle when the side rails are attached. A "V" or half-round cutout on both ends results in four feet. The rails are screwed in place, and the top is attached to the base with screws. I plugged the screw holes to keep chips and oil from accumulating in them, and I beveled all edges with a block plane before putting this horse into service.

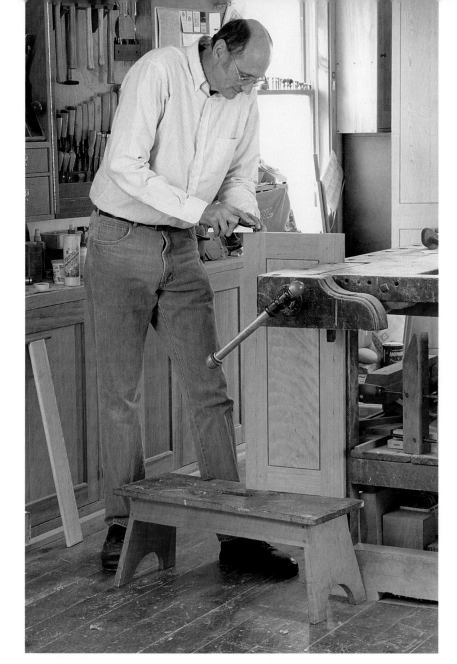

When I build a pair of these horses again, I'll make one improvement: The rails will be 4 in. to 6 in. wide for added strength and racking resistance. My set, after 22 years of use, is starting to wobble a bit. Otherwise, I'm pretty happy with them.

2-ft. Sawhorse Is the Most Useful

The 2-ft. sawhorse is the workhorse in my shop. This style is easy to make and move around. I make them in pairs, and the design allows the horses to be stacked when not in use. I also stapled carpeting to the top to prevent pieces from being damaged while they are on the horses.

Their primary use is for holding case pieces at working height. When fitting face frames, backs, or doors, or when sanding or installing hinges, I find these mid-height horses indispensable. Standing on these puppies brings me right up to the ceiling in my shop: I can change lightbulbs or sand the tops of tall cabinets. And because the braces are inboard of the legs, I can clamp onto the ends as well as the middle of the top. I sometimes use these horses to clamp case sides upright when laying out and transferring dovetails from the top to the

A PAIR OF MEDIUM-SIZE HORSES MAKES AN IMPROMPTU WORKBENCH. **At 2 ft. tall, these horses are the right height for doing finish work on a large case piece. The carpeting protects the workpiece.**

sides. This is a real handy feature when you're working alone.

There are many ways to construct a 2-ft. sawhorse. On mine, the legs are let into notches in the top piece. Braces provide racking resistance in two locations, and a shelf is handy for storage or as a step. The legs are splayed out 11 degrees to the sides. For the top, you can rip the sides of a 2x4 to 11 degrees and simply attach the legs. Or you can use a 2x6 and let in the legs. The 2x6 gives you a wider top, which provides extra stability should you wish to stand on it. In addition to having the two pairs of braces shown in the drawing, one of my 2-ft. horses has additional bracing just above the floor (see the photo above).

A shelf on the lower braces not only adds strength to the horse, but it also is strong enough to act as a lower step. The braces under the shelf provide enough support that I can stand on the shelf without it flexing. For a while I had side strips along the shelf that kept tools from rolling off. They worked, but they collected all sorts of debris and were difficult to keep clean, so I took them off.

Tall Horse Is Adjustable in Height

I recently added a third pair of sawhorses that can be adjusted in height between 36 in. and 55 in. I use these horses mainly for sanding and finishing. Even though

2-FT. SAWHORSE IS THE MOST USEFUL

This is a standard-size horse for general carpentry, but it also can be handy for holding case pieces. The shelf is optional, though it provides additional stability to the horse.

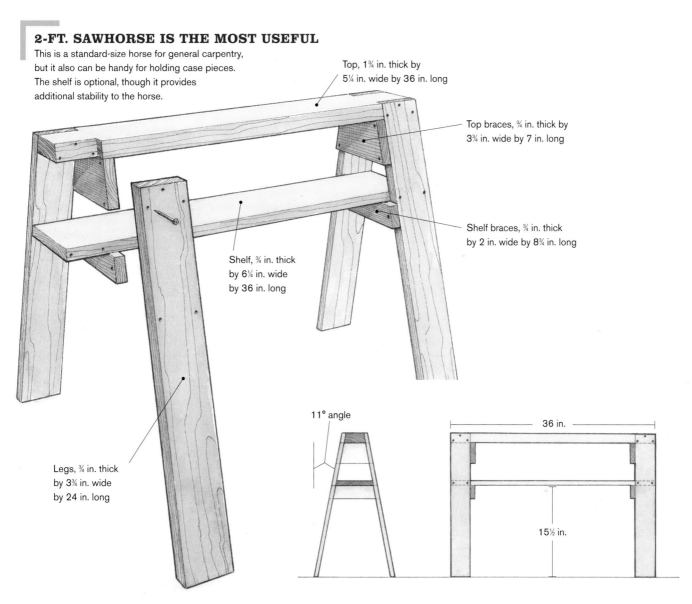

Top, 1¾ in. thick by 5¼ in. wide by 36 in. long

Top braces, ¾ in. thick by 3¾ in. wide by 7 in. long

Shelf braces, ¾ in. thick by 2 in. wide by 8¾ in. long

Shelf, ¾ in. thick by 6¼ in. wide by 36 in. long

Legs, ¾ in. thick by 3¾ in. wide by 24 in. long

11° angle

36 in.

15½ in.

they're 36 in. tall, I still have to bend over slightly, hence the extenders. For my height, 42 in. to 44 in. is ideal for sanding and finishing, especially tabletops. For fine, close-up work like carving or inlaying, I prefer 48 in. to 54 in. That's about mid-chest height for me, just right for the real fussy stuff. When I have messy work to do, I haul these horses outside, remove the extenders and use them like a bench for seat carving, grinding, sanding, and routing. At the drill press, the extenders are useful for holding long work at the correct height.

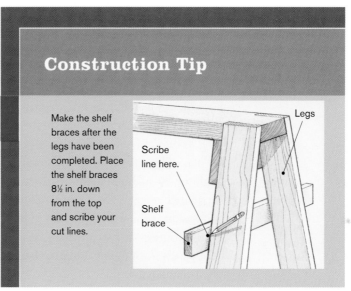

Construction Tip

Make the shelf braces after the legs have been completed. Place the shelf braces 8½ in. down from the top and scribe your cut lines.

Legs

Scribe line here.

Shelf brace

HEIGHT ADJUSTMENT IS MADE WITH A DOWEL. The holes are numbered on both sides for quick alignment.

PAD THE CROSSBARS TO PROTECT YOUR WORK. Foam pipe insulation works well and easily slips on and off the top.

ADJUSTABLE-HEIGHT SAWHORSES ARE VERSATILE. Avoid back fatigue by raising the work up to a comfortable height.

The tall horses are built almost like the two-footers. The major difference is that I have enclosed the ends and added diagonal braces for strength. The extenders consist of two 3⅝-in.-wide boards connected to a ¾-in.-thick crossbar. The boards are drilled at ½-in. intervals and fit into slots in the top and the lower shelf, much like a centerboard of a sailboat. Two ⅜-in.-dia. dowels through the ²⁵⁄₆₄-in. holes hold the extenders at the desired height. The crossbar is padded with ¾-in.-dia. foam pipe insulation to protect the workpiece. It also provides a grip to prevent panels from sliding around when they're being sanded.

Feel free to customize these horses as needed for specific applications. For example, the crossbar is fine for supporting wide panels, but it won't take the weight of a 4-in.-thick plank. A wider board or even a T-shaped crosspiece would make a good substitute. On occasion, when I use the horses as a single unit, I have scrap V boards fitted between them. Two bar clamps hold the whole unit together so that I can use it as a bench.

CHRISTIAN BECKSVOORT is a furniture maker and contributing editor to *Fine Woodworking* magazine.

The ends of the horse are made flush so that you can clamp tall pieces to them.

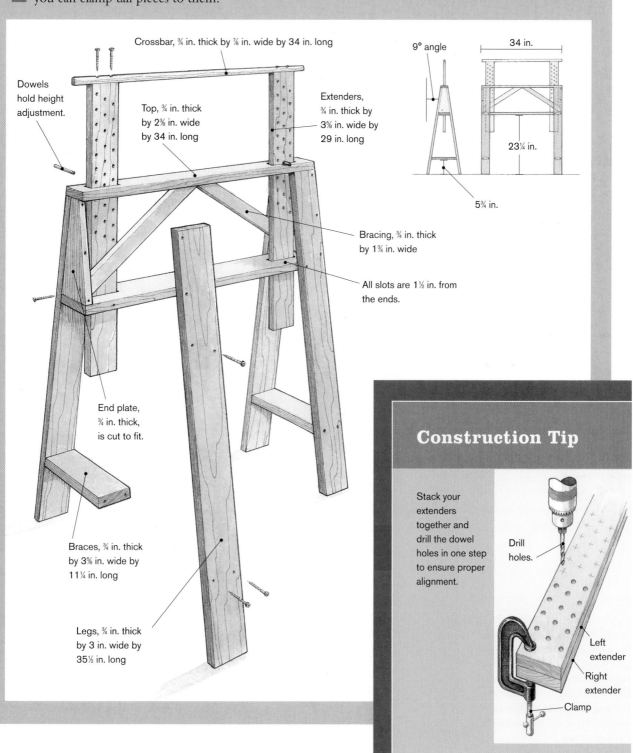

Crossbar, ¾ in. thick by ⅞ in. wide by 34 in. long

Dowels hold height adjustment.

Top, ¾ in. thick by 2⅜ in. wide by 34 in. long

Extenders, ¾ in. thick by 3⅝ in. wide by 29 in. long

9° angle

34 in.

23¼ in.

5¾ in.

Bracing, ¾ in. thick by 1¾ in. wide

All slots are 1½ in. from the ends.

End plate, ¾ in. thick, is cut to fit.

Braces, ¾ in. thick by 3⅝ in. wide by 11¼ in. long

Legs, ¾ in. thick by 3 in. wide by 35½ in. long

Construction Tip

Stack your extenders together and drill the dowel holes in one step to ensure proper alignment.

Drill holes.

Left extender

Right extender

Clamp

Making a Case for Dovetails

BY CARL DORSCH

**FOR PRACTICE CUTTING DOVE-
TAILS,** this cabinet with drawers
is a great project. Through dovetails join the carcase while
tapered, sliding dovetails secure
the shelves and vertical dividers.
The banks of graduated drawers
include lots of through and half-
blind dovetails.

When I needed a tool cabinet, I saw it as a great opportunity to practice cutting dovetails. The cabinet I designed features through dovetails, half-blind dovetails, and tapered, sliding dovetails. All of these joints can be cut either by hand or by machine; I cut mine by hand except for the tapered, sliding dovetails, which I cut with a router (see the sidebar on p. 108).

Because my cabinet in the photo below has doors, it protects the tools from dust and curious visitors, yet it leaves them readily available. The upper portion of the cabinet displays my antique planes. The shelves are spaced to hold the handplanes upright, and the cabinet is deep enough so that two planes fit side by side. The bottom of the cabinet contains several drawer banks for storing accessories and other tools.

Building the Carcase

The carcase sides are joined to the top and bottom with through dovetails. I cut the dovetails with the tails on the sides and the pins on the top and bottom so that the mechanical lock of the joint resists the weight of the cabinet and its contents. I used stopped, tapered, sliding dovetails for the shelves and drawer dividers, because I prefer them functionally and aesthetically. The taper makes this strong joint easy to assemble, as discussed in the sidebar on p. 108, and stopping the dovetail leaves a cleaner appearance than exposed joinery.

After cutting the tapered, sliding dovetails, but before assembling the carcase, I trimmed the back of the shelves to provide space for the flush back. The back of the top section of the cabinet must be rabbeted to accommodate the inset cabinet back and the hanging cleat.

Drawer Construction

The drawers have through dovetails at the back and half-blind dovetails up front. Instead of installing the bottom in grooves in the sides and in the front, I screwed them to the assembled drawers and extend them past the sides to create slides that ride in dadoes routed in the carcase sides and dividers, as shown in the drawing on p. 109. The bottom drawer in each bank slides on the shelf beneath it. I leave the bottoms slightly wide until the drawer bodies are attached, and then I plane each one to fit its dado.

Tapered, Sliding Dovetails with a Router

Sliding dovetails provide extremely strong carcase joints. But the wider the stock, the more difficult it is to slide home a straight dovetail because glue tends to bind and grab the tight-fitting pieces. By tapering one side of both pin and socket, the joint remains loose as the two pieces are assembled, until the pin is fully seated in the socket.

The trick is to get a matching taper on the pin and the socket for a perfect fit. To ensure an identical taper, I use the same ⅟₁₆-in.-thick shim for routing first the socket and then the pin, as shown in the drawing below. I cut the tapers on the upper edges of the dove-tails; the straight bottom edges of the dovetails then serve as references to ensure that the shelves are flat, square and evenly spaced.

Routing the Sockets

When routing tapered, sliding dovetails, the socket stock (cabinet sides) and pin stock (shelves) must be the same width, or the tapers will not match. Trim shelves to accommodate cabinet backs after routing the mating sockets and pins.

Routing a tapered dovetail socket requires three passes. For ¾-in.-thick stock, make the first pass with ⅜-in.dia. straight bit to hog out most of the waste. For the second pass, use a ½-in.-dia. dovetail bit, and cut a typical straight dovetail socket. The final pass with the same dovetail bit, but with the guide fence shimmed at a slight angle, routs the socket's tapered top edge.

First and second passes: Clamp guide fences A and B to the cabinet component to align the cutter with the dovetail layout line and use this setup for both passes; one with straight bit, one with dovetail bit.

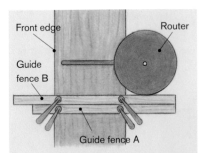

Front edge
Router
Guide fence B
Guide fence A

Third pass: Leave guide fence A clamped in place, and insert a spacer and a shim between fence A and B. The spacer determines the width of the socket (use a ⅛-in.-thick spacer for ¾-in.-thick pin sotck). The ⅟₁₆-in. shim creates the taper angle.

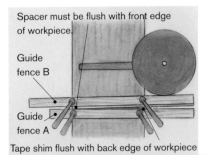

Spacer must be flush with front edge of workpiece.
Guide fence B
Guide fence A
Tape shim flush with back edge of workpiece

Routing the Pins

The pins are cut in two passes using the same dovetail bit as for the sockets but in a table-mounted router. The tapered pin side is cut in all stock before resetting the fence to rout the straight pin side. Be sure to rout a tapered side on some scrapstock to test fence setup for routing the straight side.

First pass: Adjust fence so that the dovetail bit protrudes ³⁄₃₂ in. Tape a ⅟₁₆-in.-thick shim flush with rear edge of workpiece and high enough to clear router bit.

Second pass: Adjust fence so that the dovetail bit protrudes ³⁄₃₂ in. Tape a ⅟₁₆-in.-thick shim flush with rear edge of workpiece and high enough to clear router bit.

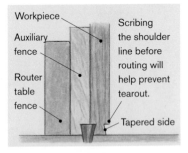

Workpiece
Auxiliary fence
Router table fence
Scribing the shoulder line before routing will help prevent tearout.
Tapered side

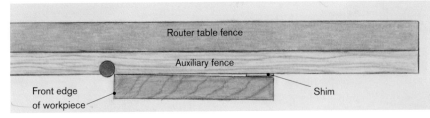

Router table fence
Auxiliary fence
Front edge of workpiece
Shim

Making and Fitting the Doors

The doors are typical frame-and-panel con-struction and overlap where they meet at the cabinet's center. To accommodate the overlap and to keep the gap between the doors centered, I made the center stile of the left door ¼ in. wider than the center stile of the right door. Both of these stiles are rabbeted to make the lap joint.

Because the knife hinges that I used to mount the doors have no provision for

A Dovetailed Tool Cabinet

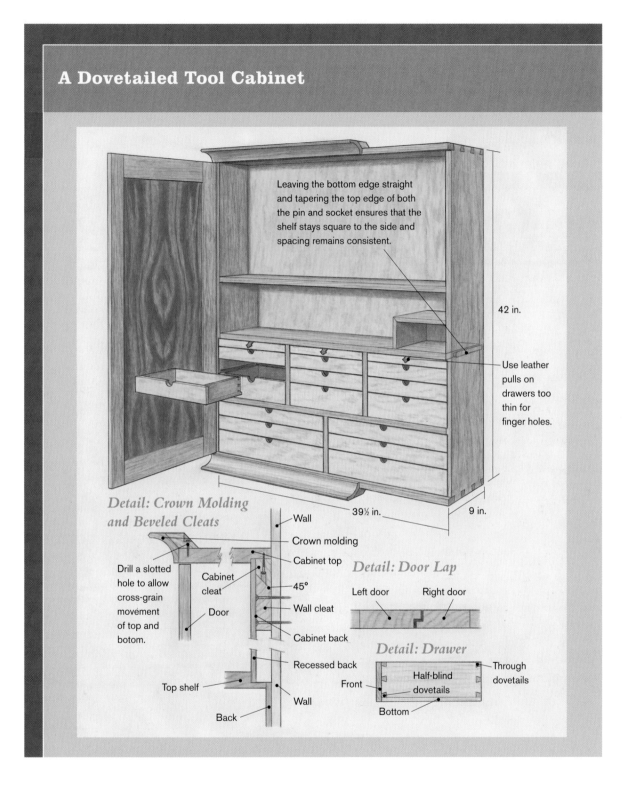

Leaving the bottom edge straight and tapering the top edge of both the pin and socket ensures that the shelf stays square to the side and spacing remains consistent.

42 in.

Use leather pulls on drawers too thin for finger holes.

39½ in.

9 in.

Detail: Crown Molding and Beveled Cleats

Drill a slotted hole to allow cross-grain movement of top and botom.

Wall

Crown molding

Cabinet top

Cabinet cleat

45°

Wall cleat

Cabinet back

Door

Recessed back

Top shelf

Wall

Back

Detail: Door Lap

Left door

Right door

Detail: Drawer

Through dovetails

Half-blind dovetails

Front

Bottom

adjusting the doors' fit, they must be accurately mortised in place. I've found that by mounting the hinges to the doors first and leaving the hinge mortises in the carcase slightly short, I can chisel out the mortises to sneak up on a perfect fit.

The cabinet can be set on a bench or hung on the wall. I hung mine on the wall using beveled cleats, one on the rear of the cabinet and one on the wall. When using this hanging system, fasten the wall cleat with two screws into each stud.

CARL DORSCH is a woodworker in Pittsburgh, Pennsylvania.

Making a Machinist-Style Tool Chest

BY RONALD YOUNG

Fashioned after the old-style machinists' boxes, this small tool chest provides convenient, portable storage for your finest tools, instruments, rules, and other small items. The original machinists' chests were traditionally made of walnut or fumed oak. I made mine of oak and stained it to match the rich brown tone the old-timers achieved through the chemical reaction that occurs when oak is exposed to ammonia fumes. The stack of graduated drawers helps prevent small objects from being inextricably buried at the bottom of the box. A separate door can be locked, covering the drawers for security during storage. The door also keeps the drawers from falling out when you're carrying the box from job to job. When you're using the box, the door slides neatly into the chest under the bottom drawer, as shown in the photo on p. 112.

My 18-in.-wide by 10¾-in.-high tool chest suits my space and storage requirements, but you should modify these dimensions and the drawer configuration to suit your particular needs. I used ⁹⁄₁₆-in.-thick oak for most of the chest. The drawer backs and sides are ⁵⁄₁₆-in.-thick poplar, and the back panel and drawer bottoms are ¼-in.-

thick oak-veneer plywood. All the hardware for my chest came from Constantine's (see "Sources" on p. 112). I suggest buying your hardware before you begin construction, so you can be sure you've dimensioned the chest appropriately.

The main body of the chest is a dovetailed box, which I constructed using a

ALTERNATE CONSTRUCTION METHODS

The basic tool chest shown here can be enhanced by using different construction techniques. Here are just a few of the possibilities.

Fig. 2: Frame and Panel Door

A frame-and-panel door dresses up the plain box and reduces the chances of the door warping or sticking with humidity changes.

FIG. 1: A MACHINIST-STYLE TOOL BOX

Using the simplified construction techniques illustrated here,
you can build this tool chest in a weekend.

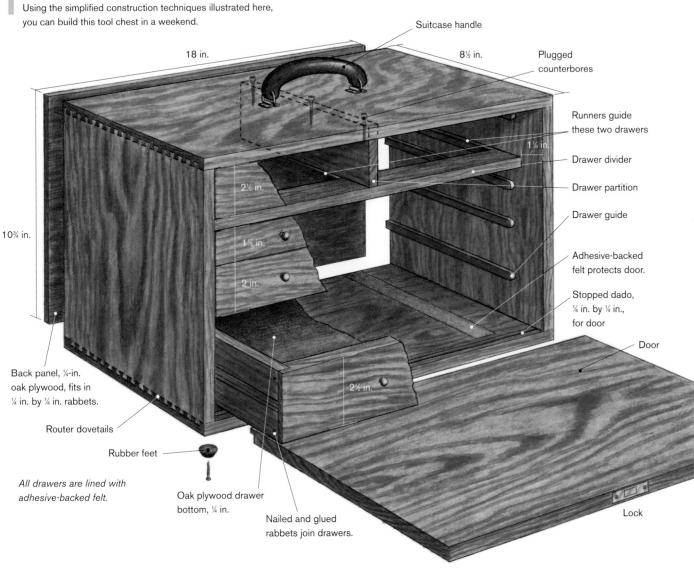

Suitcase handle

18 in.

8½ in.

Plugged
counterbores

Runners guide
these two drawers

1⅛ in.

Drawer divider

2½ in.

Drawer partition

Drawer guide

1⅛ in.

10¾ in.

2 in.

Adhesive-backed
felt protects door.

Stopped dado,
¼ in. by ¼ in.,
for door

Door

Back panel, ¼-in.
oak plywood, fits in
¼ in. by ¼ in. rabbets.

Router dovetails

Rubber feet

2½ in.

*All drawers are lined with
adhesive-backed felt.*

Oak plywood drawer
bottom, ¼ in.

Nailed and glued
rabbets join drawers.

Lock

Fig. 3: Back Panel

The back panel can be a single panel
(raised or flat) fitted into grooves in the
case sides, or it can be a frame-and-panel
assembly.

Fig. 4: Alternate Drawer

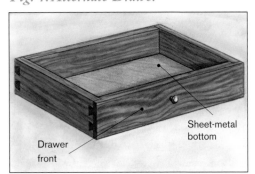

Sheet-metal
bottom

Drawer
front

Dovetailed drawers enhance the quality of the chest.
Felt-covered, sheet-metal drawer bottoms make for
a lighter box.

A MACHINIST-STYLE TOOL CHEST is a perennial favorite for storage of treasured tools because the stack of felt-lined drawers provides easy access and a safe haven.

Sources

Constantine's
2050 Eastchester Road
Bronx, N.Y. 10461
212-792-1600

commercial dovetail jig and ¼-in.-dia. dovetail bit. You could tablesaw finger joints instead, or you could use this project as a great opportunity to practice hand cutting dovetails.

Constructing the Carcase

After selecting the stock for the carcase, lay out and cut the pieces to size, as shown in figure 1 on p. 111, selecting the best wood for the top and sides. You will assemble and disassemble the parts several times while cutting the dovetails and constructing the chest, so be sure to mark the pieces on the inside faces to prevent layout mistakes.

After cutting the joints, dry-assemble the four sides, and check for square fit. Disassemble and cut the back-panel rabbets in the top, bottom, and sides. Because I ripped the rabbets on my tablesaw, I had to fill the gaps that resulted in the dovetail joints with small blocks of wood during final assembly. Using a plunge router, I cut a stopped dado along the front edge of the case bottom for the door. Although I chiseled out the mortises in the carcase sides for the drawer divider, it would have been as easy to cut them with the plunge router. Next, you should cut out the drawer partition, and

then lay out and attach the drawer guides and runners with glue and small brads to the drawer partition and the carcase sides, as shown in figure 1 on p. 111. The drawer divider is cut to size, tenoned, and screwed to the drawer partition.

A final dry-assembly lets me check the sides, divider, and runners for square before I bore and counterbore holes for the drawer partition to the carcase top. If everything is square, I cut and fit the plywood back. I then disassemble and reassemble the chest with glue, screws, and clamps (checking for square as I go) and allow the assembly to dry overnight.

Making the Drawers

Drawer construction is straightforward with simple butt and rabbet joints, as shown in figure 1 on p. 111. Be sure, however, to cut the drawer-slide grooves slightly oversized to allow for smooth movement. I did mine with a dado head on my tablesaw before assembling the drawers. A little paste wax or paraffin on the drawer runners contributes to smooth operation.

Finally, cut and fit the door, mortise the lock, and attach a suitcase handle to the top. A large chest might be better off with a handle on each side. To finish the chest, I rubbed on two coats of Watco® Danish oil and then sprayed two coats of Deft® spray polyurethane on the exposed surfaces. And to protect my finest tools, I lined the drawers with adhesive-backed felt.

Because of the simple construction shown in figure 1, I was able to build this chest in a couple of days. If you would prefer a less plain-vanilla chest, you might want to consider using some alternate construction methods, as shown from left to right in the bottom drawings on pp. 110-111. These techniques will probably take you a little longer and call for a little more material.

RON YOUNG is a woodworker in Decatur, Alabama.

Fine Furniture for Tools

BY STEVEN THOMAS BUNN

I wanted a toolbox that was both visually striking and had a lot of storage space. Appearance was a prime consideration because as a one-man shop, I can't afford to keep finished work around as showpieces, and piles of wood or half-finished parts are not impressive to a drop-in client who isn't familiar with cabinetmaking. I needed a toolbox that, like the journeyman's boxes of old, was an advertisement and demonstration of my capabilities.

I like the European-style toolbox that hangs on the wall with tools hung neatly inside. However, I don't like the large volume of wasted space behind the closed doors. In addition, the sheer number and weight of tools I possess ruled out a box that could be hung on the wall. I like the out-of-sight storage of drawers, similar to a mechanic's toolbox. I also like the idea of grouping similar tools in a single drawer so that I can pull out a drawer of chisels or gouges, set it on my bench, and then go to work. Also, drawers keep sawdust and wood chips from accumulating over my tools.

Incorporating drawers meant the cabinet needed to be relatively deep: I calculated about 17 in. deep to be effective. For both design and practical reasons, I decided to put the tool chest on its own stand, as shown in the photo on p. 114. The cabinet

and stand offer exceptional storage capacity for fine hand tools at a height that keeps me from having to reach up or bend down to get to anything. But with some slight modifications of the interior storage arrangements, the tool chest could easily house linens, china or electronic equipment. In fact, my tool chest is an interpretation of the Gate's sewing cabinet shown in *Measured Shop Drawings for American Furniture* by Thomas Moser (Sterling Publishing Co., Inc., N.Y.; 1985).

Building the Carcase

The solid panels of the case top, sides, shelves and bottom are all made of ¾-in.-thick stock, as shown in the drawing on p. 118. After preparing the stock, I routed stopped dadoes into the side panels for the shelves and bottom, guiding the router against a fence. To ensure that the dadoes were aligned, I clamped the sides together with the back edges butted against each other. I positioned the fence, squaring it to the front edge of one of the side panels, and clamped it in place.

After the dadoes had been routed into the sides, I joined the top and sides of the carcase with through-dovetails and then dry-assembled the joints. Once satisfied with the fit of the dovetails, I cut a rabbet

on the inside back edge of the top and sides for the back. The rabbet in the top was stopped at each end and squared up with a chisel. I then reassembled and glued the dovetails. The bottom was sprung into its dadoes, aligned 1 in. behind the case front to allow for the bottom face frame, and screwed into place with glue blocks from underneath, as shown in the drawing.

The shelves were driven in from behind with taps from a dead-blow mallet. The front of the shelves were notched to fit tightly against the case side and hide the dadoes. I left a ⅛-in. gap at the back of all the shelves as a safety measure in case of unequal expansion in the sides and shelves. So if the shelves swell more than the sides, the shelves won't break out the back of the case. Only the bottom was left full depth to

provide a place to anchor the board-and-spline back. The interior shelves also stop 3 in. shy of the front to leave room for the tools hung on the inside of each door.

Slide-in Drawer Dividers

Four vertical drawer dividers slide into dadoes routed in the two top shelves to form the drawer support system, as shown in the drawing. Before installation, I cut matching dadoes in all four dividers to make the drawer-guide grooves. I made a series of grooves at 1¼-in. intervals. The idea is that you could make drawers in 1¼-in. increments for greater storage flexibility. Using this modular system, you could take out two 1¼-in. drawers and replace them with one 2½-in. drawer. I've found this doesn't work in the real world. I'm not

SHOP OR HOME FURNITURE?
This tool chest could be equally at home in the parlor with just minor changes to the interior to accommodate china, silver, or even stereo equipment.

OVERSIZED STORAGE HOLDS BIG ITEMS. This two-drawer box slides into place between the shelves to hold long items that don't fit in the smaller drawers.

PREVENTING DOOR SAG. Legs screwed to the doors' lock stiles help support the heavy tools hung on the doors and prevent the hinge screws from pulling out.

leading edge. The unglued shelf is free to float in its dado behind the locking screw. The two center dividers were added last, from the back of the cabinet.

All drawer parts were batched together and cut at the same time. I built the drawers, wherever possible, from wood scrap, except the drawer fronts, where I attempted to cut all three fronts in a row from the same cherry board for grain matching. The drawers were half-blind dovetailed at the front and through-dovetailed at the back, as shown in the drawing.

Before final glue-up, I cut the groove for the drawer bottom in the sides and fronts on the tablesaw. The back was trimmed, as shown in the drawing on p. 118, so that the drawer bottom extends past the back and can move with the seasons. Planning the drawer bottom so that just the right amount protrudes lets the bottom act as a stop against the cabinet back when the drawer is closed.

After final fitting of the drawers to their openings, I glued strips to each side. The strips act as drawer runners, and they fit into the grooves cut into the vertical drawer supports.

The two longer drawers below the main drawer section are housed in a separate box, which was an addition that I made later to store tools like rulers and oversized screwdrivers.

Board-and-Spline Back for Seasonal Movement

The back is made from seven boards (see the drawing). A ⅛-in.-wide by ½-in.-deep groove was cut into both edges of five of the boards and only one edge of the remaining two boards. The two boards with only one groove were glued on their ungrooved long edges to the case-back rabbet. The remaining boards were screwed to the case top and bottom with a ³⁄₁₆-in. gap between each board. Splines were slid into

about to start making new drawers to replace ones that I already have, and changing the drawers around makes finding tools a guessing game. But beyond that, I'm tired of always being asked, "How come there are more grooves in the dividers than drawers?"

The two outside drawer dividers were installed first. Then I locked the shelves in place with one screw at each end of the shelf, driven through the carcase sides from the outside, as shown in the drawing. The counterbored and plugged screw was centered in the shelf about 1 in. behind the

SUPPORTING HEAVY LOADS. Corner braces reinforce the mortised-and-tenoned rail-to-leg joint and enable this elegant base to support the heavy tool chest.

the grooves from the bottom edge of the case until they butted into the rabbet at the top of the case. These splines float freely in the grooves with enough leeway to allow for seasonal expansion. A small brad was driven through a drilled hole in the center of each spline at the carcase base to keep the splines in place.

Legs Support the Frame-and-Panel Doors

Two frame-and-panel doors were made and fitted flush with the front of the case. I added a drop-down leg to the back of each door's lock stile to support the weight of the opened doors and the heavy tools stored on them, as shown in the photo on p. 114. The legs are short enough to fold up and stow out of the way so that the doors

close freely, as shown in the photo on the facing page. A lock and strike plate were mortised into the lock stiles and a keyhole cut in the face of one door. I had planned to add wooden doorknobs to the completed case, but the two plain doors were so striking without them that I never added the knobs. I use the key in the keyhole to open and close the case.

Base Puts Chest at Convenient Height

A four-legged base, 28 in. high, was made to hold the chest, so I don't have to bend over to get to my tools. The chest sits on the rails, and cove molding glued to the top edge of the rails hides the joint between the chest and base. The chest is not screwed to the frame; its weight is sufficient to keep it

TOOL CHEST AND BASE

All stock is ¾ in. thick unless otherwise noted.

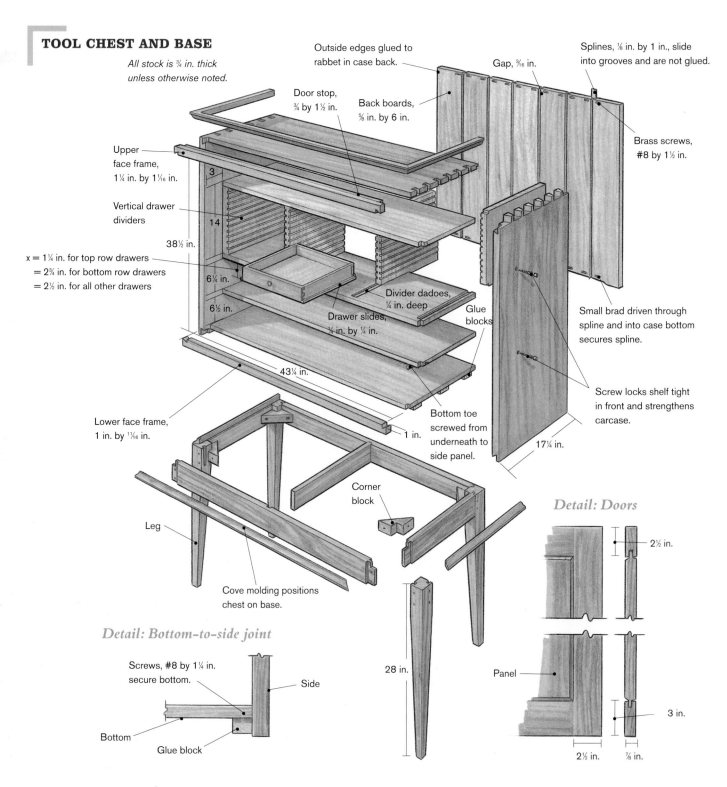

Outside edges glued to rabbet in case back.

Gap, ³⁄₁₆ in.

Splines, ⅛ in. by 1 in., slide into grooves and are not glued.

Door stop, ¾ by 1½ in.

Back boards, ⅝ in. by 6 in.

Brass screws, #8 by 1½ in.

Upper face frame, 1¼ in. by 1¹⁄₁₆ in.

Vertical drawer dividers

3

14

38½ in.

x = 1¼ in. for top row drawers
  = 2¾ in. for bottom row drawers
  = 2½ in. for all other drawers

6¼ in.

6½ in.

Divider dadoes, ¼ in. deep

Drawer slides, ½ in. by ¼ in.

Glue blocks

Small brad driven through spline and into case bottom secures spline.

Screw locks shelf tight in front and strengthens carcase.

Lower face frame, 1 in. by ¹¹⁄₁₆ in.

43¼ in.

1 in.

Bottom toe screwed from underneath to side panel.

17¼ in.

Corner block

Leg

Cove molding positions chest on base.

28 in.

Detail: Doors

2½ in.

Panel

3 in.

2½ in.   ⅞ in.

Detail: Bottom-to-side joint

Screws, #8 by 1¼ in. secure bottom.

Side

Bottom

Glue block

from moving. The legs were tapered on a bandsaw and cleaned up on the jointer. Corner blocks strengthen the base and add support for the tool chest, as shown in the photo on p. 117.

I have been using this chest for the past six-and-a-half years and am very pleased with it. The only thing I would change is the excessive number of drawer slide grooves in the drawer dividers. I also have considered replacing the stand with a lower case for storing items like routers and drills. But this one looks just too nice to change.

STEVEN THOMAS BUNN is a woodworker in Bowdoinham, Maine.

A Chisel Cabinet

BY FRED WILBUR

Early in my career as a carver, I learned the frustration of a bench cluttered with tools. As most woodworkers know, spending time trying to find the right tool when you're in the middle of a complicated project is not an efficient way to work. Invariably, I found that the less-used tools migrate to the edges of the bench, where they are more likely to fall off and then require resharpening. Having suffered such disarray, I finally gave in to the wisdom of orderliness, confessing, as did Benjamin Franklin, "I found myself incorrigible with respect to Order; and now I am grown old, and my memory bad, I feel very sensibly the want of it." What makes this sense of order more imperative as one grows older is that the problem gets worse year by year, as you collect more tools.

Whether you are a carver with a collection of gouges or a cabinetmaker with scores of chisels and screwdrivers, the ultimate storage solution is a wall-mounted cabinet near your workbench.

Cabinet Details for Strength and Convenience

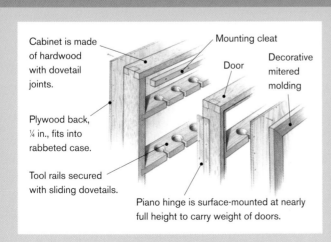

Cabinet is made of hardwood with dovetail joints.

Mounting cleat

Door

Decorative mitered molding

Plywood back, ¼ in., fits into rabbeted case.

Tool rails secured with sliding dovetails.

Piano hinge is surface-mounted at nearly full height to carry weight of doors.

DRILL AND COUNTERSINK IN ONE SHOT. With a standard shop grinder, an inexpensive spade bit can be shaped with a profile that will drill and countersink a hole at the same time.

ACCESS SLOTS MAKE IT EASY TO SLIP TOOLS IN AND OUT OF STORAGE. A small piece of wood indexed into the miter-gauge fence makes the repetitive cuts quickly and accurately.

I made this cabinet from scraps many years ago. The drawing on p. 119 shows the construction details, which afforded 183 spaces for gouges and chisels. It did look a little ridiculous at first—sheltering only a few gouges—but I have filled it up so that there are only a few vacancies left. Easy to construct, this wall-mounted unit is a shallow box with several horizontal dividers, or rails, secured with sliding dovetails. Two

doors of exactly the same shallow depth echo the cabinet carcase. By using the inside of the doors for storage space, I doubled the cabinet's capacity.

The rails have holes to hold all of my chisels and gouges. Because the various handles weren't all the same shape, I found that a countersunk hole would best accommodate the tools in an upright and tidy position. Some handles had to be shaved

slightly to fit snugly. I modified a spade bit so that I could drill and shape the counter-sunk holes in one drill-press operation. Then I cut slots in all of the holes using a finger-joint-type jig. I mounted doors to the carcase with piano hinges to carry all of the weight and used magnetic catches to hold the doors shut.

I always intended to add some pierced carvings on the front of the doors but have only applied bead-and-billet molding around the edges of the door panels. I'm sure Ben Franklin died with a few things left undone.

FRED WILBUR is the author of *Carving Architectural Detail in Wood*, published by The Guild of Master Craftsmen.

Tool-Cabinet Design

BY CHRISTIAN
BECKSVOORT

I built my toolboxes right when I got
out of high school, with only the
materials at hand, no thought to joinery
and little thought to layout. So for years I'd
worked out of boxes made of fir plywood
and knotty pine and held together with
nails, glue and barn hinges. Over the years,
my tool collection had grown until I had
planes, chisels and saws sitting on top of,
next to, and underneath the boxes. I needed
a new toolbox.

Having 30 years' experience, I knew
what I wanted and didn't want. Like most
woodworkers, I'd developed habits and
preferences. I am a furniture maker, not an

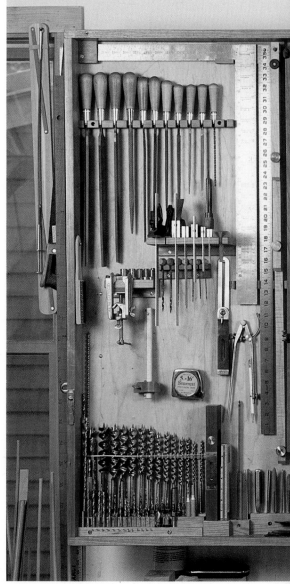

itinerant carpenter. I don't take tools to job sites, and I'm definitely not going to sea. For my purposes a tool chest was useless. I didn't want to take out three trays to reach the fourth. As in a chest freezer, the items in the bottom get lost and forgotten. I wanted to see my tools and be able to reach them with a minimum of contortions and movement of other tools. I didn't want a rolling tool cabinet, nor did I want one that looks like a piece of furniture or a building. I wanted a wall-hung box behind my workbench: simple, accessible, open and totally utilitarian.

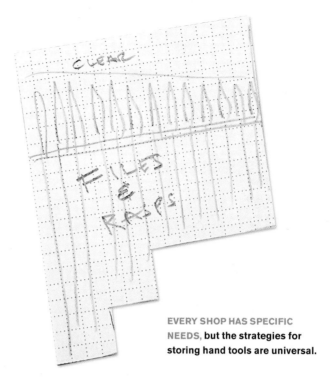

EVERY SHOP HAS SPECIFIC NEEDS, but the strategies for storing hand tools are universal.

Draw All of Your Tools to Scale

MEASURE THE TOOLS. Begin by measuring all of the tools to be housed and draw them to scale on graph paper.

ARRANGE CUTOUTS. Sort tools by type and begin to lay them out in the imaginary toolbox.

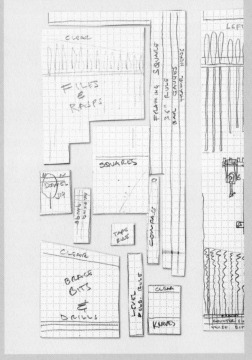

Your needs and preferences are likely to be different, but the process of planning and layout will be similar to what I went through when building the cabinet shown here. My point here is to help you through the planning process and layout. The actual dimensions and building decisions—such as materials and joinery—are yours to make as you see fit.

My design is based on a Shaker toolbox at Sabbathday Lake, Maine. It's a large, relatively shallow, wall-mounted box with framed doors for additional storage. With the design in mind, the first order of busi-

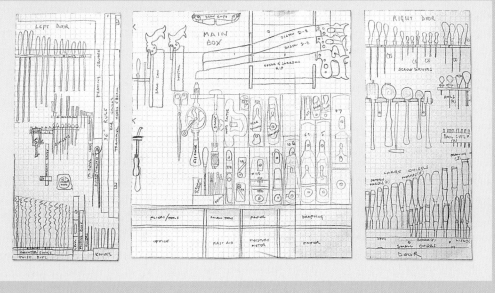

DETERMINE THE SIZE OF THE BOX. Once tools are laid out, overall dimensions are determined, and the box begins to take shape.

ness was to determine the layout of the tools for the most efficient use of space and size. I could have placed my tools all over the shop floor and regrouped them until I found the most efficient layout. That would have been pretty time-consuming, so I opted for graph paper instead (¼ in. = 1 in.).

When possible, I grouped the tools into a single cutout. Drill and brace bits fit into a 10-in. by 12-in. area, while my multitudes of chisels required a space 18 in. by 21 in. For the cutouts to be accurate, I had to start thinking about methods of hanging or storing the tools.

For example, if the chisels were to sit on a rail and be held with magnets, they could be removed straight out. However, if they were to fit in a slotted block, I would need 2 in. to 3 in. of clearance above the chisels so that I could remove them from the block. So the cutouts had to include clearance space above the tools, where needed.

It was pretty easy to group chisels, files, knives, squares, and drill bits—even planes and most saws—together on the cutouts. However, some tools, such as the brace, drawknife, scissors, straightedge, and framing square, needed individual cutouts. When designing the cabinet, you should consider saving room for tools you plan to get. Are you a chisel junkie? Would you really like to have that new Lie-Nielsen No. 10¼ rabbet plane? If so, make allowances in the chisel- or plane-group cutouts.

Once I had a little stack of odd-shaped, labeled pieces of graph paper, I started sliding them around to see how things fit. I kept related tools close to one another: chisels and mallets together, all saws and planes together and all of the diverse measuring and layout tools near each other. More shifting of patterns. I arranged the tools into a rough rectangular form and started visualizing the main box in the center, with the doors on both sides. Planes and saws, as well as other heavy, bulky tools, got moved into the main box. Layout tools, chisels, files, bits, and shallow and lightweight tools fit best in the shallow doors.

At this point, overall size became a consideration. I had my tools arranged in an acceptable manner. The chisels, slated to go into the door, were the widest group at 21 in. So with a little fudging and two ¾-in.-thick frames, I made the doors 22 in. wide. That meant that the main box would be 44 in. wide and a whopping 88 in. overall when open.

The height was more difficult to pin down. From my layout, I had one door at 44 in. high, the other at 48 in. high and the box at 35 in. high. I wanted a few drawers at the bottom of the box for pliers, punches, glass cutters, papers, drafting supplies, moisture meter, carving tools, and other little-used tools. The overall height of your cabinet will depend on your own height. The taller you are, the higher you can reach. I can easily reach 7 ft. into the toolbox. I also wanted 10 in. of clearance between the counter and the toolbox. With a little more fudging and rearranging, I settled on a height of 47 in. It accommodated the drawers and tools in both doors, was slightly taller than wide, and seemed to allow for a bit more tool collecting.

Determining the depth of the box and the doors took a little work. Decisions needed to be made on how the tools would be stored. I also needed to visualize drawer depth and how far certain groups would stick out from the surface of the doors or box. The shelf for my small squares was only 7 in. wide but protruded 6 in. from the inside of the door. I estimated the drawer depth and the angle of the plane tray and settled on a box depth of 11 in. and a door depth of 4 in., both including ⅝-in.-thick panels.

It helped me to visualize in three dimensions, so I redrew the arrangement of the tools on three sheets of graph paper: the two doors and the main box, with all of the tools and drawers in place. I knew I wanted the drawers to be flush, with ½-in. protrusions for the pulls. So the bottom 10 in. of both doors needed to have ½ in. of clearance. Above that, most of the interior of the box was empty, allowing mallet heads, squares, and chisel handles to stick out into space.

Once I had a layout that worked well, I built the toolbox with drawers and doors.

Storage Solutions for Tools

HANDPLANES

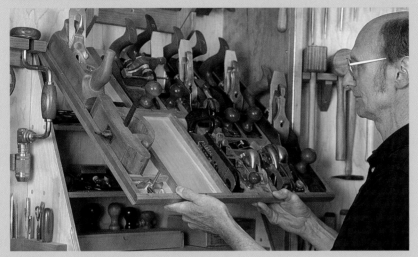

PLANES WITHIN EASY REACH. Ledger strips locate planes on the shelf, and small pieces of leather are used to protect the blades.

Planes take up a fair amount of space, no matter how you store them. But you have several options to make them accessible.

Believe it or not, many woodworkers like to hang planes vertically. A wooden plane can be fitted with a screw eye in the end and hung from a hook. For a metal plane, a fitted ledger strip will support the weight at the bottom. A similar strip with extra clearance is fitted at the top end. To remove, slide the plane upward (hence the clearance) until the nose comes out of the bottom ledger, and pull the plane forward and down to clear the bottom and then the top ledger. Or you may opt for a fitted ledger on the bottom only and a high-power rare-earth magnet near the top. Of course, this won't work for wood or bronze planes.

To save space you can also store planes on their sides, on fitted shelves. With the judicious use of dividers, the planes can be fitted into the appropriately sized rectangular shelf case. Short planes will fit front to back, and longer ones go in sideways.

I chose to store my planes on an angled tray with small (½-in. by ⅝-in.) ledger strips between them. The tray is angled at 60 degrees so that a strip in front of each plane is all that's needed to keep the tools in place. The tray is hinged at the top and has three shelves inside. I don't like to waste space, so I store seldom-used items in there: spare parts, blades, and fences. The tray needs to be emptied to gain access, because the 17 planes stored on it probably weigh close to 40 lbs.

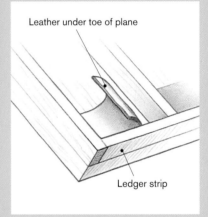

Leather under toe of plane

Ledger strip

FITTING A TOOL. Odd-shaped tools, such as this side rabbet plane, fit into french cutouts in the shelf.

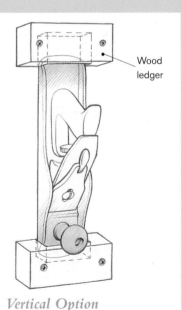

Wood ledger

Vertical Option
Clearance in the top ledger allows you to lift up and remove the plane easily. The bottom ledger supports the plane.

CHISELS

hisel storage devices are easy and relatively quick to build. Chisels are all the same shape but different in width and thickness. Sets can be stored together, graduated from the shortest to the tallest. Here are three commonly used alternatives.

Many woodworkers hang their chisels, but I'm not in favor of this method. I don't like to have razor-sharp edges exposed to fingers or other nearby tools. My current favorite method for chisel holding is a wood strip dadoed to accept chisels of various widths. Vary the spacing between narrow chisels, to allow clearance for the handles. As the chisel blades become wider than the handles, the spaces get narrower. All chisel slots are a bit wider than the blades. A 1½-in. to 2-in. strip is all that's required to hold the chisels upright. That requires only 2 in. to 2½ in. of clearance over the tops of the chisels in order to pull them out.

Another option is to use a rabbeted wood shelf at the bottom to support and protect the blades. Vertical divider strips determine the spacing of the chisels. High-power rare-earth magnets hold the chisels upright and in place. The magnets will have to be drilled into a horizontal

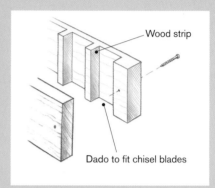

Wood strip

Dado to fit chisel blades

strip to allow clearance for the chisel handle against the panel.

In my previous toolbox I used leather straps to hold the chisels. They can be used above and below or with leather on top and a wood strip below.

TIERED CHISELS. Inside the door, chisels are stored in dadoed strips to protect their cutting edges.

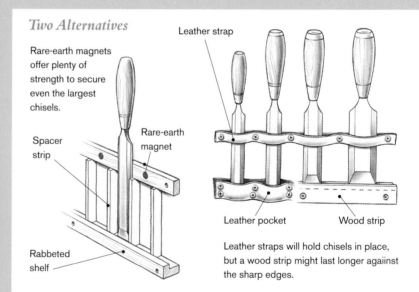

Two Alternatives

Rare-earth magnets offer plenty of strength to secure even the largest chisels.

Spacer strip

Rare-earth magnet

Rabbeted shelf

Leather strap

Leather pocket

Wood strip

Leather straps will hold chisels in place, but a wood strip might last longer agaiinst the sharp edges.

Then I made the tool racks and hangers. As I assembled the racks and actually hung the tools, I noticed that a few had to be shifted a bit to allow for easier access. A few items were moved once or twice, until they felt right in place. The first time I tried to close the doors, I discovered that they wouldn't. The compass plane stuck out right where the two door frames came together. I shifted the planes until I got the layout I liked, then screwed the dividers into place.

SCREWDRIVERS, FILES, AND AWLS

SIMPLE IS OFTEN BEST. Awls and screwdrivers rest in holes drilled into a small shelf.

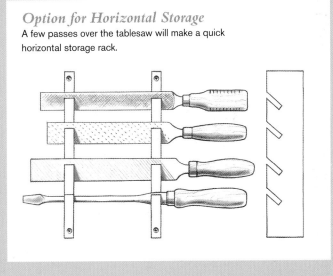

Option for Horizontal Storage
A few passes over the tablesaw will make a quick horizontal storage rack.

Screwdrivers, files, and awls can be stored like hammers. After all, they are nothing more than metal rods or bars stuck into wood handles.

My favorite method is to hang these tools. A ¾-in. by 2-in. strip of the correct length will suffice. Measure the ferrules or the base diameters of the tools, space them as needed and drill slightly oversized holes partway into the strip. Then locate the hole centers and saw a slot to the back of the hole. This yields a small

shoulder on both sides of the cut, which supports the ferrule. The slot allows for easy removal. Simply lift the tool a mere ½ in.

Files and screwdrivers with large flats on the upper shaft can be stored horizontally on racks or trees, consisting of two parallel uprights with 45-degree slots cut into them. Trees are merely uprights with holes drilled through the sides.

Like chisels, screwdrivers and files can be stored with leather retainer straps.

The layout took about 11 hours, and the case, doors and drawers took an additional 48 hours. The almost 40 racks, holders, shelves, and trays took 60 hours, and the finishing, hanging, placing, and rearranging took another 10 hours.

All things considered, the box turned out well. It works! Of course, it was months before I got used to the new arrangements. Thirty years of reaching for the tape measure on the right-hand door doesn't change overnight. A few of the lesser-used tools

LAYOUT TOOLS

Layout and measuring tools are an odd bunch, because there are so many different individual shapes. A framing square can be hung by the short leg either on a 16-in.-long strip with a groove for the edge or on two small ledger blocks—one at the end and the other right at the inner corner. The ledger strips should have small lips.

Long rulers and straightedges are most easily hung from a round-head screw through a hole in the end. Remember to hang the ruler at least ⅜ in. proud of the surface or carve finger-relief holes to make grabbing the ruler easier. The same method can be used for story sticks, trammel heads on a beam, and winding sticks.

Small squares can be stored in a variety of ways. The best-looking but most time-consuming method for any tool is the french cutout. Trace the tool onto an oversized board, then cut out the tracing with a coping saw. The tool can then be placed in its own custom-cut hole. Much faster and easier is to let the head of the square rest on a ledger strip, similar to the one used on the framing square. The method I prefer, especially with an assortment of squares, is to mount them on a 6-in.-deep shelf with slots in the front to accept the blades of each square.

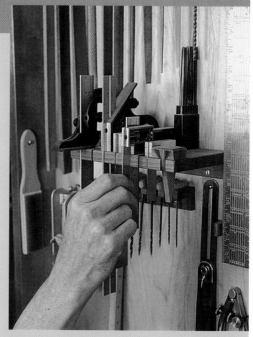

SHELVED SQUARES. Becksvoort's squares slide into sawkerfs cut on a small shelf, which takes up much less space than laying them out flat.

HANDSAWS

Handsaws are fairly easy to store. What method you choose depends on how many saws you have, how much space you have and whether you want to see the handles. The easiest method, which also takes up the most room, is to hang the saw flat, either vertically or horizontally. Make a cutout to fit exactly inside the handle hole and then screw it into place. A spinner can be added if you're worried about earthquakes or if the saw will be stored in the door of the tool cabinet. A saw can be hung horizontally from a peg, set onto a ledger or fitted to a shelf, as I did.

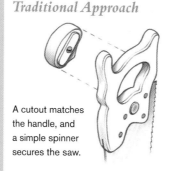

Traditional Approach

A cutout matches the handle, and a simple spinner secures the saw.

AN AESTHETIC CHOICE. Becksvoort prefers to store saws so that their shapes and engravings can be seen.

are, in fact, in out-of-the-way places. The gimlets, for example, live behind the hanging blades of the squares. But they are easy to reach, with good clearances.

Once I got everything placed and made the necessary changes, the cabinet became the centerpiece of the shop. And although the fine-tuning may still take a few more weeks, the time spent planning, laying out and anticipating paid off handsomely.

CHRISTIAN BECKSVOORT is a contributing editor to *Fine Woodworking* magazine.

An Inspired Tool Chest

BY BILL CROZIER

Between my freshman and sophomore years at the Rhode Island School of Design, I was looking ahead to the fall when I would begin studying woodworking under Tage Frid. That same summer, my father mounted a show of illustration at the New York Historical Society. The exhibition was a pretty big deal—but with precious little relevance, you might think, to woodworking. However, one evening as my father entered the Historical Society by the usual after-hours route—through a basement area stuffed with holdings in storage—he stumbled upon an extraordinary find: the tool chest of Duncan Phyfe, the New York City cabinetmaker who gave his name to an elegant style of furniture in the first decades of the 19th century. My father said he'd try to get permission for me to see it. A week later, I got my chance.

If I had seen the chest closed, I might have walked right by it. Typical of Old World-style joiner's tool chests, it was essentially a ruggedly built blanket chest with drawers and compartments inside for tools. This box had the usual simple, scuffed exterior, but when the lid was lifted, I was in for a treat. The drawer box, or till, had rows of shallow, beautifully proportioned drawers veneered with crotch Cuban

ONE FINE CHEST LEADS TO ANOTHER. Bill Crozier found an idea worth emulating when he came across Duncan Phyfe's tool chest (right) in a museum. Scottish-born Phyfe (1768-1854) established himself in New York as the pre-eminent cabinetmaker. Almost synonymous with the Federal style, Phyfe's furniture was typically made of mahogany and often finely carved with lyres, reeding, and swags. Phyfe left an estate of a half-million dollars—a sum that testifies to his popularity, his craftsmanship, and his business acumen.

AN INSPIRED TOOL CHEST comes from an inspired woodworker. Above, Bill Crozier stands proudly with a tool chest, inspired by the work of Duncan Phyfe.

mahogany and filled with scores of exquisite tools, with handles of bone or ebony or rosewood, all well used but in superb condition. The drawers were joined with flawless, tiny dovetails and sported pulls turned from elephant ivory. Below the drawers, dozens of molding planes were nested in neat compartments.

I wasn't permitted to touch the chest or the tools, but the curator who agreed to let me see them said that if I wanted anything moved I could ask the guard on duty nearby. Well, I gave the poor guy a workout. I was there the better part of a day, absorbing and drawing every detail. After sketching the cabinet construction and layout, I noted which tools were contained in each of the drawers. I took particularly careful notes because I knew that the first project in Tage Frid's curriculum was to build a tool chest, and I figured I had found a pretty good starting place for the design of mine.

In the following weeks, I worked to design my own tool chest, using Duncan Phyfe's as inspiration. What appealed to me most about his chest was the drawer till, with its pleasingly slim and perfectly proportioned drawers. I decided to make a fairly direct copy of it, adding one row of drawers. But I didn't like the idea of having to bend over to fetch my tools, and I didn't want to have to root around in a dark box, moving one tool to get to another. So for my design, I essentially lifted Phyfe's drawer till out of the big blanket chest and put it on an open stand at a comfortable height.

I followed Phyfe's lead again in turning drawer pulls in a range of sizes—larger ones for the bigger bottom drawers and smaller ones to suit the smaller drawers. I turned mine from rosewood instead of ivory. And although I loved the way the crotch mahogany looked on his drawer fronts, I chose to have solid fronts on my drawers and made them from a mixture of bird's-eye maple and tiger maple.

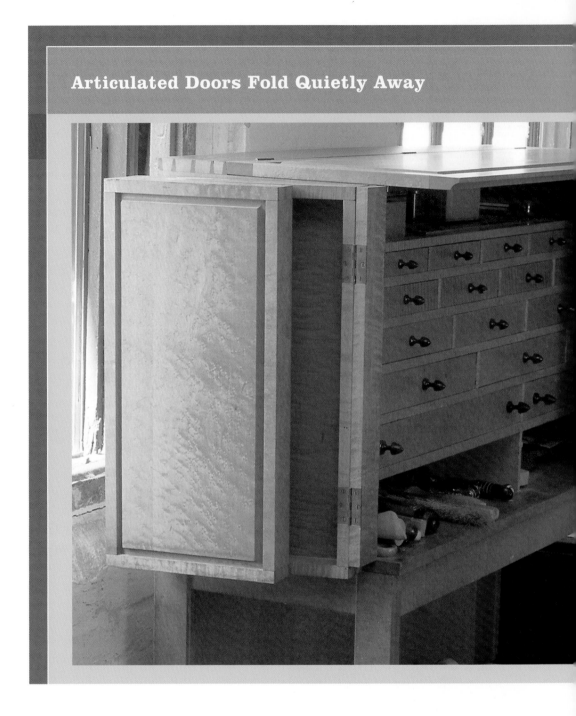

Articulated Doors Fold Quietly Away

I admired the way Phyfe used his chest as well as the way he made it. He arranged things so tools with similar functions were in adjacent drawers. I did the same thing: I keep layout and marking tools in the first row of drawers, with squares in one drawer, marking knives and pencils in another, compasses and dividers in a third. The second row is reserved for chisels, with paring chisels in one drawer, mortising chisels in the one beside it, and Japanese chisels in the next. This has made it easy to remember where things are even in a bank of 20 drawers. To protect the tools, I lined the top two rows of drawers with upholstery velvet. For the bottom three rows, I glued sheet cork in the bottoms.

I still wanted to be able to lock the chest, so I gave it a lid and built accordion-style doors that fold out of the way at the ends of the drawer box, but can be pulled across to engage the lid and lock the whole

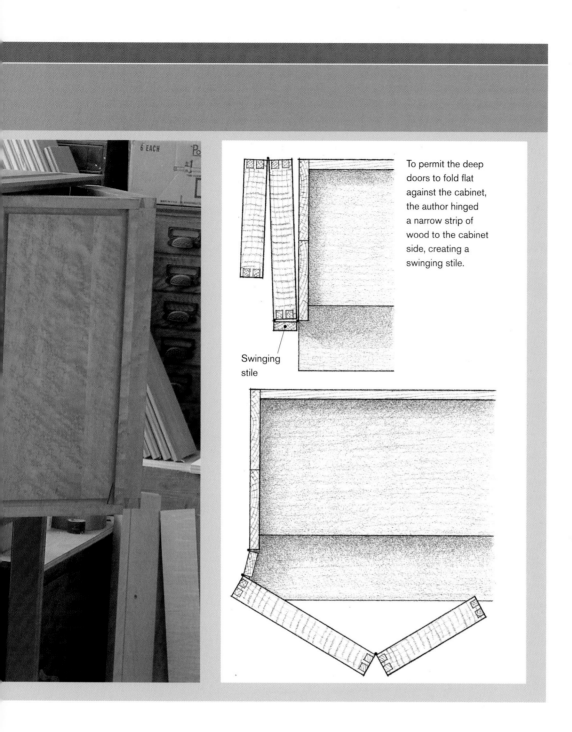

To permit the deep doors to fold flat against the cabinet, the author hinged a narrow strip of wood to the cabinet side, creating a swinging stile.

Swinging stile

thing shut. As it turns out, I never close them. But I suppose when you design something like this you are just guessing how the future will go, and you are not always right. I also left cavities below the bottom drawers for trays I envisioned as holding the day's tools. They would be easily removable so I could take them to the bench or wherever I was working. That still sounds like a good idea, but I've never made the trays. I also left a space on the

stand below the drawer box because I intended to build a case of larger drawers for power tools. Maybe I'll build it next year.

So far, I've gotten two decades of service from my tool chest. But it would have served me well even if I'd never used it, because making it was like a double apprenticeship —one in joinery and the other in design— under a pair of masters. We were asked to build our boxes using either all mortise-and-tenon joinery or all dovetails. I chose

ORGANIZING YOUR DRAWERS. The author noticed that Duncan Phyfe organized his tools by rows of drawers and followed suit. Having all the various chisels, for instance, in adjacent drawers makes it easier to keep track of them.

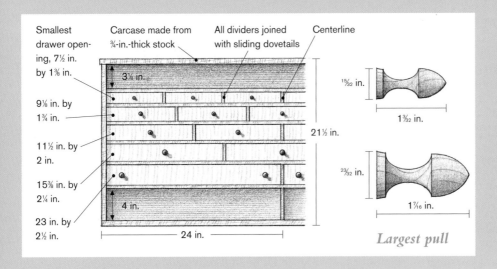

Smallest drawer opening, 7½ in. by 1⅜ in.

9⅛ in. by 1¾ in.

11½ in. by 2 in.

15⅜ in. by 2¼ in.

23 in. by 2½ in.

Carcase made from ¾-in.-thick stock

All dividers joined with sliding dovetails

Centerline

3⅛ in.

21½ in.

4 in.

24 in.

15/32 in.

1⁹/₃₂ in.

²³/₃₂ in.

1⁷/₁₆ in.

Largest pull

dovetails because I'd never cut them and was eager to try. Cutting all the dovetails in the stand, the doors, the drawer box, and the drawers themselves with Tage Frid's guidance was a real dovetail apprenticeship. And as I made my way through my first

attempt to design and build a major piece, I was also serving a design apprenticeship under the eye of Duncan Phyfe.

BILL CROZIER designs and builds furniture in Providence, Rhode Island.

Heirloom Tool Chest

BY CHRIS GOCHNOUR

A cabinetmaker's tool chest embodies a certain nostalgia and charm for modern woodworkers. It speaks of a time when craftsmen had few tools but an abundance of skill. Tool chests often served as a calling card to display a craftsman's talents. However, some were utilitarian, built simply to house tools.

The tool chest described in this article is of the latter kind—practical, enduring, and simple. But in a time when woodworkers have an abundance of power tools at every turn, making this tool chest with traditional hand-tool techniques can be a bridge to an era past. I recommend using this project as a hand-tool exercise, though power tools could be substituted for any of the operations. Practicing the techniques involved in the chest's construction will make you more confident with hand tools, and you may find them an indispensable resource in your day-to-day shop tasks.

Choose and Mark the Material

Select a medium-density hardwood that is worked easily with hand tools. Because the tool chest is intended to be carried, choose wood that is lightweight yet durable. For this box I chose cherry, which is easy to work and attractive; however, woods such as red alder, poplar, and white pine also are appropriate.

To reduce the likelihood of warp and twist, select clear, straight-grained wood for the lid frame. This type of wood also is good for the moldings because it will make them easier to work with molding planes. Knots are fine on panels, but keep them away from the edges so that they will be out of the way of the joinery.

Once you've dimensioned the lumber for each part, mark them with cabinetmaker's triangles. These triangles clearly identify the face and the inside and outside edges of each part. And they are helpful for identifying the orientation of the pieces when you begin cutting joints.

From here, follow a sequential pattern of construction: Join the box using dovetails; build the frame-and-panel lid with mortise-and-tenon joinery; shape and apply moldings; and install the hardware.

Practice and Plan the Carcase Dovetails

I tell students that making dovetails is easy, but controlling a handsaw can be difficult. Get comfortable using a handsaw before you undertake the dovetails, and practice dovetail-like cuts on scraps of wood to improve your skill.

THIS CLASSIC CHEST offers a
lesson in efficient woodworking.

Clear and accurate layout is essential to hand-cutting dovetails. Much of your success will come down to your layout and your ability to work to the lines and never cut beyond, which comes with practice. The objective is to cut precisely to the layout lines each step of the way. This will greatly minimize cleanup and fitting, making the entire process more efficient and enjoyable.

Cut the tails two boards at a time I cut the tails first and then use them to lay out the pins. I also cut the tails on the front and back of the chest at the same time with the two boards clamped together in a vise. It is faster and more accurate because the saw has a longer line to follow as you make the perpendicular cut along the end grain. Check your cabinetmaker's triangles to see whether you have oriented the boards correctly; the inside faces of the boards should be touching.

Next, remove the bulk of the waste with a coping saw one board at a time. Finally, chop to the baseline with a chisel. This is a critical step for the dovetails to fit together snug. One method I use is to guide the chisel with a block of wood clamped in place along the baseline. Chop halfway through from each side to avoid tearout.

Cut the pins to match the tails The tails on the chest's front and back boards are used to lay out the pins. With one board secured vertically in the bench vise, place the adjoining tail board on top, carefully aligned, and then secure it with a clamp.

Once again, make sure the box parts are oriented correctly, then define the pins on the end grain by tracing the tails with a marking knife. Next, deepen the marks using a broad chisel with its bevel facing the waste. This chisel mark will help guide your saw. Continue the layout line down the face of the board with a sharp pencil, stopping at the scribed shoulder line.

The pins are cut much the same as the tails; however, it is more critical here to cut to the line and not past it. With the saw resting to the inside of your chisel mark, make the vertical cuts down the waste side of the pins. Next, remove the bulk of the waste with a coping saw and pare to the baseline with a chisel.

Cut the Bottom Panel

The bottom panel of the chest must be sized and fitted prior to glue-up. The panel floats in a groove plowed on the inside of the sides, front, and back of the chest carcase. Use a mortise gauge to scribe two lines ⅜ in. apart, about ½ in. from the bottom. Now plow the groove with a plow plane. The scored lines from the mortise gauge ensure a clean cut.

The chest bottom is rabbeted, leaving a ⅜-in. by ⅜-in. tongue that will be housed in the groove. Define the rabbet with two scribe lines, then remove the material between these lines with a fillister plane. Remember, the chest's bottom panel should be free to shrink and expand in the groove. Make sure it is slightly undersize, and don't glue it during assembly.

Glue Up the Chest Carcase

Dry-fit the carcase prior to assembly to ensure that all of the dovetails fit properly and that the bottom panel has room to move. I've found that the glue-up can take some time, so an extra pair of hands and slower-setting glue can be helpful.

I prepared notched cauls that fit around the dovetail pins to spread the clamp pressure evenly without getting in the way of the joinery. Four clamps evenly spaced are adequate for each side. Make sure the chest is glued up squarely, and readjust your clamps to correct any sides that may be out of square.

A Comfortable Home for Tools

Made of cherry and constructed entirely with hand tools, the tool chest incorporates dovetail joinery, frame-and-panel construction, and applied molding.

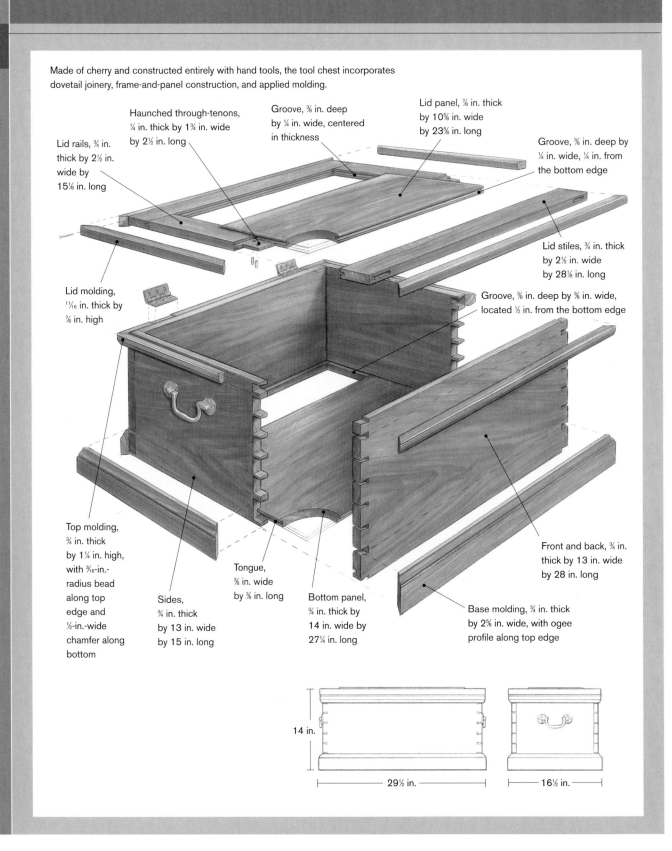

Lid rails, ¾ in. thick by 2½ in. wide by 15⅛ in. long

Haunched through-tenons, ¼ in. thick by 1¾ in. wide by 2½ in. long

Groove, ⅜ in. deep by ¼ in. wide, centered in thickness

Lid panel, ⅞ in. thick by 10⅝ in. wide by 23⅝ in. long

Groove, ⅜ in. deep by ¼ in. wide, ¼ in. from the bottom edge

Lid stiles, ¾ in. thick by 2½ in. wide by 28⅛ in. long

Lid molding, 1¹⁄₁₆ in. thick by ⅞ in. high

Groove, ⅜ in. deep by ⅜ in. wide, located ½ in. from the bottom edge

Top molding, ¾ in. thick by 1¼ in. high, with ³⁄₁₆-in.-radius bead along top edge and ½-in.-wide chamfer along bottom

Sides, ¾ in. thick by 13 in. wide by 15 in. long

Tongue, ⅜ in. wide by ⅜ in. long

Bottom panel, ¾ in. thick by 14 in. wide by 27¼ in. long

Front and back, ¾ in. thick by 13 in. wide by 28 in. long

Base molding, ¾ in. thick by 2⅝ in. wide, with ogee profile along top edge

14 in.

29½ in.

16½ in.

Dovetail and Assemble the Case

CUT THE TAILS. Clamp both the front and back of the chest in a vise with the inside faces touching (left). Make the cuts with a backsaw. Next, clean out the waste one board at a time with a coping saw (below). Make sure you do not cut past the scribe line.

CHOP TO THE BASELINE WITH A CHISEL. Use a block of wood, securely clamped along the scribe line, to guide the chisel. Chop partway from both sides of the board to avoid tearout.

MARK THE PINS WITH THE TAILS AS YOUR GUIDE.
With the tail board clamped firmly in place, trace
the tails onto the end grain of the pin board with a
marking knife. Deepen the marks with a chisel to
provide a kerf for the handsaw.

GLUE UP THE CARCASE. After
dry-fitting all of the pieces, coat
the dovetail joints with slow-
setting wood glue and assemble. The rabbeted bottom panel
floats in the grooves plowed
into the four sides. No glue is
needed.

Once the glue has dried, plane the dovetails clean and flush, and turn your attention to the chest's lid.

Through-Tenons Make a Sturdy Frame-and-Panel Lid

For the lid's frame, I used through mortise-and-tenons. Through-tenons make the lid stronger because they provide more glue surface, and the strong, long grain of the rails passes all the way through the weak cross-grain of the stiles. In this way, the tenon serves as a reinforcing cross-ply to the outside edge of the lid. Through-tenons also minimize the chance of twist in the frame. Because the mortises are chiseled out from both sides at the same point, it is impossible for the tenon to come through on an angle. Also, chopping all the way through the stile is faster because you don't have to clean the bottom of the mortise, a difficult task.

The lid should be ¹⁄₁₆ in. larger than the box on all sides to provide clearance for the applied moldings. Size your stiles and rails taking this into account. Also, overcut the stiles by 2 in. to account for horns, which add strength to the material when you're cutting the mortises. The horns are then trimmed off after the lid has been assembled.

One setting on a mortise gauge is used throughout On the inside edge of the stiles, mark each end where the rails will intersect the stiles. Then measure ⅜ in. from these lines and draw two more marks to define the width of the mortises. Because it is a through-mortise, the lines also must be transferred across the face onto the outer edge of the stile.

Set up your mortise gauge precisely to mark the groove for the lid panel as well as the mortises and tenons. Scribe all of these lines referencing off the face of the boards. Last, lay out the tenon cheeks, haunch, and shoulders with a marking knife.

Apply the Moldings

CUT THE FRONT MOLDING TO SIZE FIRST. Once the front molding has been fitted and clamped to the carcase, measure and cut the side moldings to fit. The back piece is cut and fitted last.

A VERSATILE MITERING JIG

This simple maple jig works as a miter box, accommodating a panel saw in three positions for cutting at 90° or 45° in either direction, and doubles as a miter jack. One end is cut at 45° and is designed for fine-tuning miters with a bench plane. Once you have sawn the miter, secure the workpiece in the shooting end of the jig with a cross pin and wedge, and trim it to perfection.

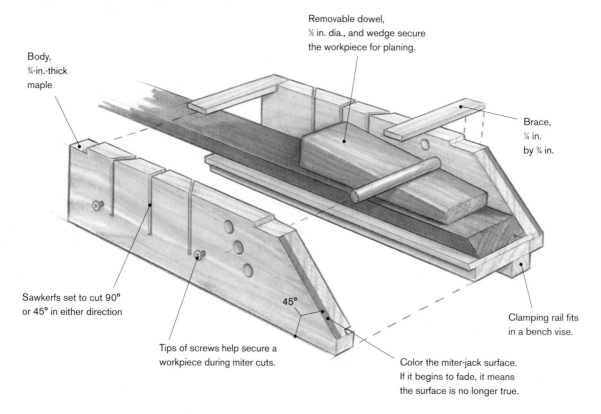

Body,
¾-in.-thick
maple

Removable dowel,
½ in. dia., and wedge secure
the workpiece for planing.

Brace,
¼ in.
by ¾ in.

Sawkerfs set to cut 90°
or 45° in either direction

45°

Tips of screws help secure a
workpiece during miter cuts.

Clamping rail fits
in a bench vise.

Color the miter-jack surface.
If it begins to fade, it means
the surface is no longer true.

GLUE THE TOP MOLDING. Later, after the hardware has been installed, nail the molding with finish nails to add more holding power.

THE LID MOLDING MASKS MINOR WARP OR TWIST IN THE FRAME-AND-PANEL. Set the lid on the box and apply the molding so that it rests on the edge of the carcase molding.

OFFSET THE MOLDINGS TO CREATE A LIPPED LID

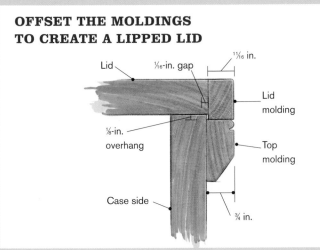

Lid

¹/₁₆-in. gap

1¹/₁₆ in.

Lid molding

¹/₈-in. overhang

Top molding

Case side

¾ in.

Rough-cut the haunched tenons and then chop out the mortises Once the lines have been marked, begin rough-cutting the tenons. Cut close to the lines, but leave material for final fitting later. Then plow the groove on the inside edge of all the stiles and rails. Be sure to reference these plow cuts off the same face of each part, guaranteeing a consistent alignment of the groove.

Finally, chisel the mortises. The key to successful mortising is to use the right chisel—one with a thick blade to keep the chisel from twisting and a long bevel to take a shearing cut. Clamp together the two stiles in a wooden hand screw with the grooves facing up. Clamping the boards will prevent them from splitting as you chisel away the waste. Work your way through half the width of the stile on all four mortises. Then flip over the stiles and finish chopping from the other side. When you are all the way through, clear out the debris and use a paring chisel to clean up any irregularities, ensuring that the mortise is straight and true on all four sides.

Once the mortises have been completed, fit the tenons. I used a paring chisel or shoulder plane to fine-tune the shoulder and a router plane set to the depth of the layout lines to fine-tune the fit of the tenons. Dry-assemble the frame, and use this as one more chance to get an accurate measurement for the panel.

Plow a groove in the panel and assemble
The panel should be sized to fit into the groove with some extra room to accommodate expansion and contraction with humidity changes. Locate and scribe a groove on the mortise gauge with the same setting as used for the frame. However, this time register off the bottom side of the panel. Then plow the groove on all four sides.

Next, shape a thumbnail molding on the panel with a block plane. Before applying

glue, dry-fit the frame and panel to make sure all the parts go together well. After gluing up the frame-and-panel lid, trim off the horns and check that the lid is square to the box and slightly oversize.

Top Off the Chest with Molding

The molding on the tool chest is not only attractive, but it also serves practical purposes. Along the bottom it provides a bumper to protect the box as it is toted from place to place. On the top, the molding seals the chest interior, keeping it relatively free from dust and humidity.

I enjoy shaping and applying the molding because I love working with molding planes, and I like seeing the box begin to take on its final form. Molding planes are simple tools, with only a contoured wooden body and a steel blade. They don't require electricity like a router does, and the only noise they make is the sweet sound of wood being sheared from a board edge in long, continuous shavings. I enjoy the slight physical workout involved when using molding planes and the satisfaction of seeing the molding emerge from the board edge. The whole process takes me back to a time when there was nothing between the board and the craftsman except a well-tuned tool.

I milled the base molding using a molding plane with an ogee profile. A cove, quarter-round, or simple bevel profile would suit the chest just as well. I shaped the molding for the upper portion of the chest with $\frac{3}{16}$-in. beading on its top edge and a bevel on the bottom. The band of moldings for the lid is shaped with $\frac{1}{8}$-in. roundover, but only after it has been applied to the lid frame.

Begin by cutting miters on the front base molding until the piece fits the carcase. Then work your way around the chest measuring and cutting the side pieces and

Make and Hang Tool Trays

The interior tool trays slide along cleats attached to the carcase sides. The sides and bottoms of the trays are ¼ in. thick. The ends of the small trays are ½ in. thick. The ends of the saw box are ¾ in. thick and notched to fit the cleat.

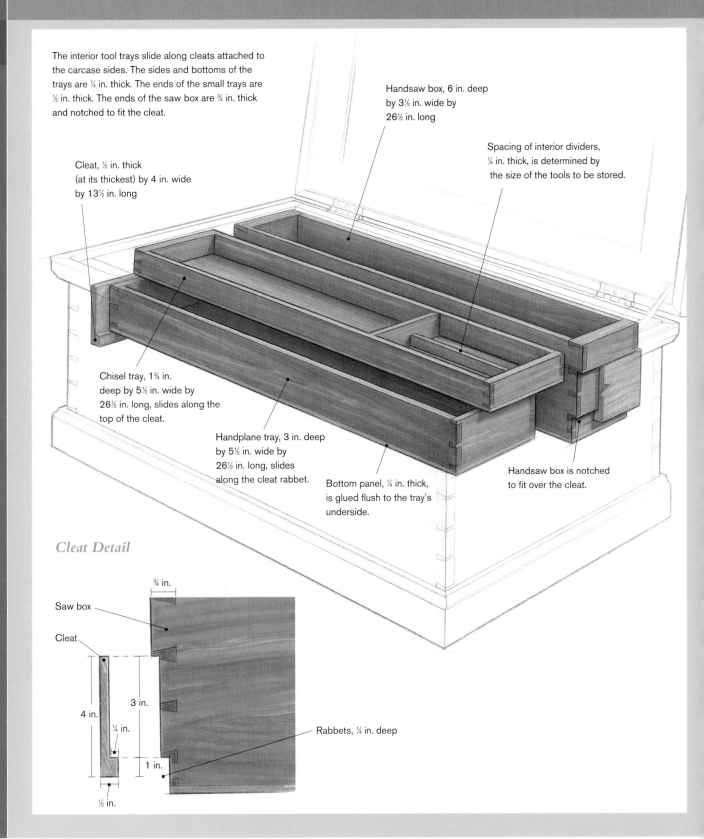

Cleat, ½ in. thick (at its thickest) by 4 in. wide by 13½ in. long

Handsaw box, 6 in. deep by 3½ in. wide by 26½ in. long

Spacing of interior dividers, ¼ in. thick, is determined by the size of the tools to be stored.

Chisel tray, 1¾ in. deep by 5½ in. wide by 26½ in. long, slides along the top of the cleat.

Handplane tray, 3 in. deep by 5½ in. wide by 26½ in. long, slides along the cleat rabbet.

Bottom panel, ¼ in. thick, is glued flush to the tray's underside.

Handsaw box is notched to fit over the cleat.

Cleat Detail

Saw box

Cleat

¾ in.

3 in.

4 in.

¼ in.

1 in.

½ in.

Rabbets, ¼ in. deep

TRAYS SLIDE ON CLEATS INSIDE THE CHEST. Nail the cleats to the inside of the chest so that the trays slide front to back. The two shallow trays should have enough clearance to slide past each other.

DOVETAILED TRAYS HOLD HAND TOOLS. The three trays are sized specifically to hold Gochnour's chisels, planes, saws, and various other hand tools. The sides are dovetailed and the bottom panels are glued flush to the trays.

finally the rear section. Carefully fit each miter joint as you move around the chest. I used a miter jack for this. Apply the moldings first with glue and clamps, and then secure them later with finish nails, being careful not to put nails where the hinges and lid stay will be installed. Follow this series of steps to install the lid and the lid moldings.

Build the Sliding Trays to Fit

Because this tool chest is such a personal item, the inner tray system can be personalized, too. I designed mine with three removable sliding trays, which hold saws, chisels, handplanes, and a host of other hand tools. The tray boxes are dovetailed, and the bottom of each tray is glued flush in place. Two stepped cleats tacked onto the inner sides of the chest support the trays, allowing them to slide forward and backward on different planes.

Install Hardware and Finish

Finish off the tool chest by installing the brass hardware, which consists of two 90-degree stopped handles, two mortised hinges, and a lid stay. The hinges are screwed onto the molding, which is why it's a good idea to reinforce the molding with a few finish nails once the hardware has been installed.

I finished the chest with three coats of Tried and True oil/varnish blend applied over several days, scuff-sanding between coats. Tool chests often get abused, so I avoid built-up finishes such as shellac or lacquer, which are prone to scratching and scuffing. But painting the chest would not be out of character with traditional tool chests. Use a flat acrylic latex paint, which imparts a look similar to milk paint, and top it off with a thin shellac topcoat.

CHRIS GOCHNOUR makes custom furniture in Salt Lake City, Utah.

The articles in this book appeared in the following issues of *Fine Woodworking*:

p. 4: Fine-Tune Your Shop by Jerry H. Lyons, issue 170. Photos by Mark Schofield, courtesy *Fine Woodworking*, © The Taunton Press, Inc.; Drawings by Jim Richey, courtesy *Fine Woodworking*, © The Taunton Press, Inc.

p. 10: Roll-Away Workshop by Bill Endress, issue 167. Photos by Matt Berger, courtesy *Fine Woodworking*, © The Taunton Press, Inc.; Drawings by Brian Jensen, courtesy *Fine Woodworking*, © The Taunton Press, Inc.

p. 17: Versatile Shop Storage Solutions by Joseph Beals, issue 105. Photos by Charley Robinson, courtesy *Fine Woodworking*, © The Taunton Press, Inc.; Drawings by Bob LaPointe, courtesy *Fine Woodworking*, © The Taunton Press, Inc.

p. 24: Four Ways to Get Organized, issue 160. Photos by Anatole Burkin, courtesy *Fine Woodworking*, © The Taunton Press, Inc., except photos on p. 24 (bottom right) and on p. 29 by Leroy Trujillo, courtesy *Fine Woodworking*, © The Taunton Press, Inc.; Drawings by Melanie J. Powell, courtesy *Fine Woodworking*, © The Taunton Press, Inc.

p. 30: Clamp Storage Solutions, issue 164. Photo on p. 30 by William Duckworth, courtesy *Fine Woodworking*, © The Taunton Press, Inc.; Photo on p. 33 by Barbara Duerr, courtesy *Fine Woodworking*, © The Taunton Press, Inc.; Photo on p. 34 by Dean Della Ventura, courtesy *Fine Woodworking*, © The Taunton Press, Inc.; Drawings by Jim Richey, courtesy *Fine Woodworking*, © The Taunton Press, Inc.

p. 36: Tilt-Top Shop Cart by Fred Sotcher, issue 160. Photos by Anatole Burkin, courtesy *Fine Woodworking*, © The Taunton Press, Inc.; Drawings by Melanie Powell, courtesy *Fine Woodworking*, © The Taunton Press, Inc.

p. 39: Stack and Saw Lumber on the Same Rack by Chris Gochnour, issue 147. Photo by Anatole Burkin, courtesy *Fine Woodworking*, © The Taunton Press, Inc.; Drawing by Bob LaPointe, courtesy *Fine Woodworking*, © The Taunton Press, Inc.

p. 42: Convertible Clamping Workstation by Gary B. Foster, issue 174. Photos by Matt Berger, courtesy *Fine Woodworking*, © The Taunton Press, Inc.; Drawings by Melanie Powell, courtesy *Fine Woodworking*, © The Taunton Press, Inc.

p. 50: Low Assembly Bench by Bill Nyberg, issue 118. Photos by Aimé Fraser, courtesy *Fine Woodworking*, © The Taunton Press, Inc; Drawings by Heather Lambert, courtesy *Fine Woodworking*, © The Taunton Press, Inc.

p. 54: Vacuum Hold-Down Table by Mike M. McCallum, issue 102. Photos by Mike M. McCallum, courtesy *Fine Woodworking*, © The Taunton Press, Inc.; Drawings by Matthew Wells, courtesy *Fine Woodworking*, © The Taunton Press, Inc.

p. 58: Rolling Chopsaw Stand Saves Space by Charles Jacoby, issue 98. Photo by Charles Jacoby, courtesy *Fine Woodworking*, © The Taunton Press, Inc.; Drawings by David Dann, courtesy *Fine Woodworking*, © The Taunton Press, Inc.

p. 62: A Downdraft Sanding Table by Peter Brown, issue 153. Photos by William Duckworth, courtesy *Fine Woodworking*, © The Taunton Press, Inc.; Drawing by Bob LaPointe, courtesy *Fine Woodworking*, © The Taunton Press, Inc.

p. 65: Power-Tool Workbench by Lars Mikkelsen, issue 101. Photo by Sandor Nagyszalanczy, courtesy *Fine Woodworking*, © The Taunton Press, Inc.; Drawings by Mario Ferro, courtesy *Fine Woodworking*, © The Taunton Press, Inc.

p. 69: New-Fangled Workbench by John White, issue 139. Photos by Jefferson Kolle, courtesy *Fine Woodworking*, © The Taunton Press, Inc.; Drawing by Jim Richey, courtesy *Fine Woodworking*, © The Taunton Press, Inc.

p. 77: A Bench Built to Last by Dick McDonough, issue 149. Photos by Tom Begnal, courtesy *Fine Woodworking*, © The Taunton Press, Inc., except photos on pp. 82–83 by Erika Marks, courtesy *Fine Woodworking*, © The Taunton Press, Inc.; Drawings by Vince Babak, courtesy *Fine Woodworking*, © The Taunton Press, Inc.

p. 86: Rock-Solid Workbench by Jon Leppo, issue 162. Photos by Tom Begnal, courtesy *Fine Woodworking*, © The Taunton Press, Inc.; Drawings by Bob LaPointe, courtesy *Fine Woodworking*, © The Taunton Press, Inc.

p. 96: Build a Better Sawhorse by Voicu Marian, issue 105. Photo by Voicu Marian, courtesy *Fine Woodworking*, © The Taunton Press, Inc.; Drawing by Maria Meleschnig, courtesy *Fine Woodworking*, © The Taunton Press, Inc.

p. 98: Sawhorses for the Shop by
Christian Becksvoort, issue 161.
Photos by Michael Pekovich,
courtesy *Fine Woodworking*, © The
Taunton Press, Inc., except photo
on p. 98 by Tim Sams, courtesy
Fine Woodworking, © The Taunton
Press, Inc.; Drawings by Heather
Lambert, courtesy *Fine Wood-
working*, © The Taunton Press, Inc.

p. 106: Making a Case for
Dovetails by Carl Dorsch, issue 96.
Photo by Carl Dorsch, courtesy
Fine Woodworking, © The Taunton
Press, Inc.; Drawings by Lee Hov,
courtesy *Fine Woodworking*, © The
Taunton Press, Inc.

p. 110: Making a Machinist-Style
Tool Chest by Ronald Young, issue
99. Photo by Charley Robinson,
courtesy *Fine Woodworking*, © The
Taunton Press, Inc.; Drawings by
Lee Hov, courtesy *Fine Woodworking*, © The Taunton Press, Inc.

p. 113: Fine Furniture for Tools by
Steven Thomas Bunn, issue 108.
Photos by Charley Robinson,
courtesy *Fine Woodworking*, © The
Taunton Press, Inc.; Drawing by
Bob LaPointe, courtesy *Fine Wood-
working*, © The Taunton Press, Inc.

p. 119: A Chisel Cabinet by Fred
Wilbur, issue 149. Photos by
William Duckworth, courtesy *Fine
Woodworking*, © The Taunton Press,
Inc.; Drawing by Michael Gellatly,
courtesy *Fine Woodworking*, © The
Taunton Press, Inc.

p. 122: Tool-Cabinet Design by
Christian Becksvoort, issue 153.
Photos by Michael Pekovich,
courtesy *Fine Woodworking*, © The
Taunton Press, Inc., Drawings by
Michael Gellatly, courtesy *Fine
Woodworking*, © The Taunton Press,
Inc.

p. 131: An Inspired Tool Chest by
Bill Crozier, issue 132. Photos by
Jonathan Binzen, courtesy *Fine
Woodworking*, © The Taunton Press,
Inc.; Drawings by Vince Babak,
courtesy *Fine Woodworking*, © The
Taunton Press, Inc.

p. 137: Heirloom Tool Chest by
Chris Gochnour, issue 169. Photos
by Matt Berger, courtesy *Fine
Woodworking*, © The Taunton Press,
Inc., except photo on p. 138 by
Michael Pekovich, courtesy *Fine
Woodworking*, © The Taunton Press,
Inc.; Drawings by Bob LaPointe,
courtesy *Fine Woodworking*, © The
Taunton Press, Inc.

The New Best of Fine Woodworking series

A collection of the best articles from the last ten years of Fine Woodworking.

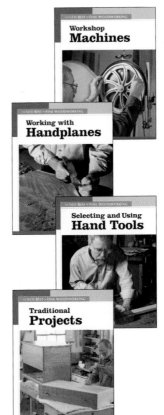
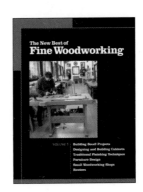